THI$ CHANGE$ EVERYTHING

THE ABSOLUTE, INDISPUTABLE, FASTEST WAY FROM ZERO TO WEALTH!

Terry Kennedy & Don Spini

Copyright © 2020. All rights reserved.
This book, or parts thereof, may not be reproduced in any form without the written permission from the author; exceptions are made for brief excerpts used in publication reviews.

Printed in the United States of America

ISBN: 9798612898382

10 9 8 7 6 5 4 3 2-

EMPIRE PUBLISHING

www.empirebookpublishing.com

ACKNOWLEDGEMENTS

We would like to acknowledge the following people, for whom without their support, this book would not have been possible.
To our incredible team that took the bull by the horns and turned our rough concept into a powerful, yet simple to follow testament to our life's work. This team is led by Logan Marcus and Tana Shivers.

To Logan Marcus, our General Counsel, legal eagle, and co-editor, your attention to detail is unmatched. Your ability to wordsmith without losing our voice throughout this arduous process was truly amazing. You inspire us to be better people every single day.

To Tana Shivers, our public relations guru and co-editor, we sincerely appreciate your dedication and commitment to our cause. You fill a need in the promotional and public relations space that we are simply in awe of.

To Amanda Kennedy, our strength, our impetus, your drive, vision, and professionalism are the standard for which all should strive. Your wisdom is exceptional beyond your years.

To our beautiful children, six daughters in all, you each have captured your dads' hearts forever.

ABOUT THE AUTHORS

Terry Kennedy is a longtime Las Vegas native and the President and CEO of Appreciation Financial, a full-service national financial powerhouse with headquarters in Las Vegas and an Inc. 5000 company two years in a row (2018 & 2019). Focused on providing solutions for all areas of life, including insurance and retirement planning, the birth of Appreciation Financial happened in a classroom. After seeing teachers fall victim to bad financial advice, Kennedy decided to educate the educators about protecting their hard-earned investments. That personal mission led him to start Appreciation Financial in 2008. In the years following, Kennedy has visited more than 1,000 schools and has personally helped nearly 2,000 teachers plan for a vibrant life after the final bell rings. While Appreciation Financial offers a conservative product for those who can't afford to lose money, Kennedy's goal for the company is anything but conservative. After meeting with so many teachers, his passion for giving back to those who give so much to our community grew. As Kennedy explains, "Appreciation is not just our name - it's a way of doing business. Giving back in the communities where we do business is a cornerstone of our company."

Kennedy feels very strongly about the people he serves, "Our clients are public servants. They are educating our future leaders, pushing through government red tape to get the best outcomes possible for their communities, and even saving lives. I have a service-driven life mission to help the helpers. It feels great to help these amazing individuals protect their future and families."

Kennedy is the recipient of the 2019 Gold Stevie Award for Entrepreneur of the Year-Financial Services from the American Business Association. He is also a 2019 finalist for the Ernst & Young Entrepreneur of the Year Award.

Kennedy resides in Henderson, Nevada with his wife, Amanda, and their four daughters.

Don Spini is a nationally recognized speaker and best-selling author. For over 25 years, Spini has led numerous successful national sales teams for Fortune 500 financial organizations. After retiring from corporate America in 2009, he made the decision to share his sales methodology for free with entrepreneurs and sales professionals throughout Orange County, California. What Spini didn't anticipate was the overwhelming response he received regarding his methodology. This prompted him in 2010 to write his book "60-Seconds to Yes", which immediately became a national best-seller.

Since the success of "60-Seconds to Yes", Spini has been asked to speak at national sales conventions around the country while also coaching and training some of the most successful professionals in the financial services industry and beyond. Spini's true passion is helping sales professionals achieve their dreams and aspirations by following his simple system that can create life-changing wealth for anyone. This desire was the impetus for Spini conducting over 150 full-day workshops per year, from 2010 to 2014, making him one of the most prolific sales trainer in the country.

Currently, Spini is the Chief Sales Officer and Chief Operating Officer of Appreciation Financial, a national financial services company dedicated to serving teachers, public employees, their families, and friends. Spini has dedicated most of his career to building and leading national sales teams, mostly in the financial services industry.

Spini lives in Las Vegas, Nevada, and Scottsdale, Arizona, with his WWII veteran father, his youngest daughter, and his fiancé.

Contents

Preface 1

Chapter One
    The Most Insane Game Ever Played 5

Chapter Two
    The Hunt Begins Here 11

Chapter Three
    The Painful Truth. 25

Chapter Four
    The Trinity of Success 29

Chapter Five
    The Greatest Chapter in the History of Books 35

Chapter Six
    Giving and The Give Back Strategy 51

Chapter Seven
    The Three Agreements and Your Word 63

Chapter Eight
    "BombShelly" 75

Chapter Nine
    The Five Absolutes of Wealth 85

Chapter Ten
    Final Thoughts 93

Reference 95

Preface

Terry Kennedy and Don Spini always joke that it took 25 years of combined experience to become "overnight" successes.

Read that carefully: It took them 25 years! You don't have to experience the same level of failure and frustration that they did to become a success because they have written this book for you!

Within the pages of this book hold what Terry and Don truly believe is the quickest way to a six, seven, and even an eight-figure a year income. They not only believe this - they can prove it!

Wherever you are in your personal and professional journey, we encourage you to execute the simple plan outlined in this book, and it will work for you as it did for them. Nevertheless, it is important to understand this plan does not act as a magic wand; you must still do your part and put in the hard work to become a success. We know that you have always been willing to work hard and work smart, but the major issue standing between most people and success is simply a lack of knowing what to do to achieve it.

In addition, you probably did not have a proven, viable, and tangible system to use in conjunction with your hard work to attain the success you have been seeking.

That changes now - because this book changes everything!

Before we begin, check in with your mindset to make sure you are ready to commit to this process. It may seem cliché to state the obvious, that you "need to be positive" because everyone already knows that. Although positivity is crucial, this book will put you in a drastically different mindset: the unwillingness to fail.

Once you are unwilling to fail and have a system to succeed, you will be on the path to success.

The war against failure is over, and now is the time to use the system we have outlined in this book to collect the spoils of that war.

The following three requirements are necessary to get started:

- A passion for helping others before yourself.
- A simple business idea with a product or service that speaks to that passion.
- A lake to fish in – a clearly identifiable place to find the people you can help.

If you already have even one of these requirements, you are ready to begin. As you read this book, you will see the simplicity of our methods, and by the end, you will possess all three.

Ready? Let us begin…

Chapter One

The Most Insane Game Ever Played

Terry tells a particular story at every one of his training and speaking events that has been truly life-changing for many! To this day, many of the people who launched successful businesses after attending one of Terry's training or speaking events look upon hearing Terry's story as the pivotal moment where things changed.

The story goes like this:

"I was living in Las Vegas bored one afternoon, so I decided to head down to the local casino to kill some time and play the tables. I walked inside and headed back towards the gambling hall. Blocking my way to the tables was a large crowd gathered in front of me. I could tell by the energy in the room that the crowd was mesmerized by something. What were they all watching?

Needing to see for myself what had captivated all these people, I politely worked my way through the crowd towards the front. When I finally got there, I quickly understood why the spectators were so intrigued.

Before me stood a standard blackjack table. It was like any other ordinary blackjack table with six seats and a dealer. As you know, the table rules are usually printed and on display for all players to see. Typically, there is a small placard that contains the table information, i.e., the minimum bet, maximum bet, and explanations for side bets. However, after a moment of closer observation, I noticed that this table had one unbelievable difference.

It had no printed rules and no placards! Instead, the table rules hung above it, in the form of a giant neon sign, visible for the entire casino floor to see. I read the rules and immediately understood why the crowd was so large. I, too, could not believe my eyes!

The rules read as follows:

Rule #1 – Bet as much money as you want on any hand!

Rule #2 – If you lose, you keep your money! (*What*?)

Rule #3 – If you win, you keep your winnings!

Three simple rules! Wait a gosh darn minute! "There must be a mistake," I thought to myself! "How could this possibly be true?"

Wouldn't you have the same thoughts if you stumbled across this game yourself? I hope you are sitting down because what you are about to read next will surely weaken your knees.

Given the nature of the rules at this table, one would think that all the seats would be taken, and there would be a line around the entire casino of people waiting to play!

Much to my surprise, only five seats out of the six were taken, leaving an empty seat at the end! Was there a waiting list? Could it be that there was an invisible line? None of this made sense to me.

I asked the Pit Boss if there was a wait to get a seat at the table. He replied, "Nope. No waiting, that open seat is available". I looked back in amazement and saw hundreds of people still watching the game. If everything I saw was true, how could there possibly be a seat available? Did these people see something in the rules that I was missing?

The Pit Boss continued, "There is always a seat available. In fact (he pointed behind him to an open floor full of empty tables), see all these empty tables? We are always ready and willing to open another table if more people want to play this game."

I looked behind the Pit Boss and indeed saw the room was full of empty tables and chairs. I asked the woman standing next to me why she was not playing. "There must be a catch," she replied. The crowd around us heard her response and nodded in agreement. Well, now my skepticism started to rise as well!

Maybe this woman was right. Maybe there was a catch! I stood there, watching for a little while longer.

Then, I decided. Later I would look back and come to realize that this was the single most important decision I had made in my life up to that point. I decided to take a chance and sit in the empty seat, expecting the "joke" to be on me, and for the "catch" to become apparent immediately.

Out of courtesy for the other players, I asked if they mind that I join the table. I feared there was only so much that could be won, and I didn't want to take away from those who had been gutsy enough to take the leap of faith before me. After all, I was the Johnny-come-lately who had to observe them all first before taking the same risk. To my surprise, they all smiled in unison, and warmly welcomed me to the table.

I pulled out a little bit of money to start with, still expecting the practical joke to reveal itself to me at any moment. Keep in mind, like many people who might find themselves in this same situation, I was nervous. It took a great deal of courage for me to sit down in front of this large crowd, none of whom had been brave enough to take the empty seat as I had. Suddenly, I started to feel like the proverbial "sacrificial lamb".

With a little bit of hesitation, I placed a small bet on the table. Go figure, I lost. To my astonishment and disbelief, the dealer did not take my money but instead pushed the bet back towards me. *It happened*, I thought to myself. *It happened just like the rules said it would! How was this possible?*

My interest piqued, so I bet a little more on the next hand. I lost, and again the dealer pushed my bet back towards me. Slowly my confidence started to rise, so I upped my bet, and this time I won. The dealer matched my bet with the casino's money, pushing my bet and the winnings back to me! Unbelievable, right?

As I looked around the table, I noticed all the players had huge stacks of chips in front of them, which must have been worth a fortune. We were all experiencing the same phenomenon. The rules were legitimate! It! Was! Working!"

This story is relevant because Terry and Don have since been at that very same "table" for over a decade, making millions in such a simple way. Most importantly, they have been fortunate enough to share the opportunity to sit at that very same table with so many of their friends and family. We are all winning at the same game together.

As I'm sure you've surmised by now, the casino described in Terry's story is a metaphor for life.

Life, like a casino, is a giant room full of people, all looking for a chance to win. Life and casinos give us all the opportunity to win or lose big. It is always up to us to take the first step.

Walking through the door is certainly an essential first step, but that alone does not provide any guarantee of winning.

In order to win in both life and business, we need to fully understand the game we are playing. We also need to break the game down into its simplest terms to understand the rules.

Furthermore, once we understand how to play, we need to have the courage to enter the game. If we do not enter the game, or take that empty seat, as Terry did, we will never have the chance to win.

Remember all the spectators in the story who were standing around the table too afraid to take a seat and join the game? All of these people thought there must have been some kind of "catch" to the rules of the game, which prevented them from even taking a chance. Maybe they thought the game might be too difficult to play, or that the entry fee to play must be too high, and therefore the risk was too great to be worth the possible benefits.

What if entering the game required very little investment and very little to no risk? Would you be more willing to join the game then? Absolutely, you would be. The table described in this chapter is the game of life as it pertains to sales and business, and it represents the system we are going to develop and present to you in this book.

If you follow our system and stay the course, you simply cannot lose, and you will already be in a much better position to win, and to win big!

You may ask, "*Why does the game work?*" The game works because of the 'law of abundance,' which states that there is no limit to how much wealth can be achieved, no limit to the amount of money and riches one can amass, and no limit to the number of people that can benefit from the game. The opportunities and possibilities of the game are endless!

In the next chapters, we will give you the equipment and strategies necessary to play big in the game of life. Once you read this book, you will understand the game clearly and know how to play it to win.

Disclaimer: As we teach our system in the pages of this book, you will be asked to think differently. You will learn to set goals, plan, take specific actions, invest in, believe in, and be accountable to yourself, and most importantly, step up to the winner's table and take your seat!

Chapter Two

The Hunt Begins Here

Whenever you embark on a new venture, you need to begin at an identifiable starting point. For you, that starting point is right here, and right now.

We would like to begin this chapter with an important question. Did you know that being in sales and becoming an entrepreneur puts you at the top of the wealth food chain? Entrepreneurs play a fundamental role in society and always have. Since the beginning of civilization, it is these people who have created all the goods and services bought and sold. They were the first small business owners and laid the groundwork upon which we have built our system.

Let's look at a parallel concept in nature.

There are three types of hunters in the animal kingdom. There are also three types of hunters in the world of business and entrepreneurship. In nature, the hunters are at the top of the food chain.

In the animal kingdom, we find the scavengers at the bottom of the food chain. These are animals that wait for something to die so that they can eat it. They are often passive and take no true proactive action to feed themselves. Some of the most notable animals that fall into this category are vultures, hyenas, and coyotes.

Scavengers typically hunt in packs and, therefore, must share their food with others. As a result, they are always hungry. They exist in a constant state of scarcity, meaning there is never consistently enough food to go around, and no one is ever satisfied.

You see, the scavengers are the least-skilled hunters. In general, when they hunt, they tend to make a lot of noise squawking and howling. Nothing sabotages hunting more than noise because noise scares other animals away. Noise repels prey. Read that again carefully; noise repels prey!

Who are these so-called scavengers in the world of business? They are the unskilled, uncommitted, and unaccountable salespeople who give an entire industry a bad name and reputation. These scavengers earn this reputation because they are always trying to take shortcuts at their clients' expense, with the end goal being a large commission payment. They may start with pure intentions, but frustration from their lack of success will soon either drive them out of the business, or lead them to commit unscrupulous business practices to make money. The problem is that these scavengers have tried every "trick" in the book. They waste their money buying training methods, which teach manipulative practices. They chase internet promises at a great expense to their already dwindling cash reserves. They fall for more of the false promises offered from social media advertising, "guaranteeing" success with no real tangible or duplicatable system.

Because the scavengers do not know the established methods you will discover in this book, they instead "hope" things will just "work out" for them. We all know this never really happens. In general, these are the same people who are not willing to put in the hard work, dedication, and discipline necessary to make their business successful. "Hope" is not a successful strategy for a business, and these scavengers are often left bitter and broke.

As they burn through their warm market contacts of family and friends, they eventually discover their approach is ineffective, even on the people that support them the most. How discouraging it must be to know that your own mother won't buy from you? Soon they have nowhere else to turn after these markets dry up. They are left with little to no confidence in their abilities, their products, services, or opportunities.

In fact, most of these same people find themselves out of business, blaming their failures on anything and everyone else around them, other than themselves. Remember, the scavengers genuinely believe that they have already tried everything to become successful. The reality is that most of these people wasted their time looking for a magic pill that simply does not exist - a genie in a bottle that would provide instant success upon a wish.

Folks, there is no magic pill. There is no genie in a bottle. You won't need a magic pill if you follow our system!

To summarize the plight of the business scavenger, their obvious lack of skill repels potential clients, which leaves the scavenger salespeople perpetually hungry, like their animal counterparts. Why does this happen? Because they are doing it wrong – they make too much noise!

Understand that sometimes the business we decide to enter may repel clients by its nature alone. Network marketing is a prime example. It is a great business model with an immense amount of value, but the general public is wise to the decades of manipulative techniques that have tarnished this business. We all know the name most people give the network marketing industry - 'pyramid scheme'.

Yet, we also know that most businesses operate in a multi-level capacity. Society seems to accept a large, well-established corporation or bank which pays their top executives a lot of money from the efforts of others at the middle and the bottom of their corporate structure. However, when it comes to individuals who try to build their own empire in the same fashion, it is insinuated that there must be something manipulative about the way they built their empire. How is that fair?

This preconception plays into the mindset of any new person hoping to join an organization as well. It is hard to escape the negative connotation of being in a multi-level opportunity. It's OK. We can also help you with this and show you ways to prevent these negative connotations from affecting your business! There will be more on that later.

The following section of this chapter may be shocking to you, so please pay close attention. The next category of hunters in the wild is the predators, like the big cats. Who are these predators in nature? They are smart, strong, and fast. They may operate alone or in packs; either way, they experience a much higher rate of success than scavengers. Because they do not make unnecessary noise, predators can get very close to their prey. Due to their higher skill level of hunting, predators operate in complete silence, until it is too late for their prey, and then the chase is on.

In business, the idea of being a big cat is sexy and exciting. Everyone thinks they want to be the "tiger" or "lion" in their respective fields. We get it. The largest crowds at the zoo seem to converge around the big cats.

Before you adopt the predator's strategy as the right strategy for you, let's ask ourselves a question; "What is the number one cause of death for big cats in the wild?"

Starvation.

You see, chasing prey is a waning and diminishing skill. Predators age and do not remain as fast and skilled at catching their prey forever. They will eventually weaken and wither away, dying from starvation.

Now, who are the predators in the business and entrepreneurial world? They are the flashy salesperson who can sell anything to anyone. They are the person everyone always describes as being able to "sell ice to an Eskimo." The predators use their charm, charisma, and sleight of hand to get what they want in business and life. They generally make a lot of money, and they lose a lot of money. The problem is charm and charisma can only take you so far in the world, especially if you have no real substance behind it.

Predators often die alone and broke.

For the predatory salesperson, the game, chase, and hunt are the draw. They do not honestly believe in the products or services they are selling; they solely focus on how much they can manipulate and ultimately attack their prey.

To the predator, sales is all just a numbers game. They use other people as a means to an end. People are mere pawns that help them get to the "platinum" level in their organization and may lead to fancy trips to exotic destinations. Their clients are not real people to them with names or families; they are just simply another line item on the way to achieve their quotas.

It may be surprising to know that the primary goal of a predator is not to build a lasting business with perpetual residual income. Perhaps it is not internally all their fault. Maybe they started with the right mindset and good intentions. Although, one thing we do know is that the road to hell is paved with good intentions!

The good news is this is not you, nor will you become like this. You are not a predator.

Now let's reveal the hunter with the highest skill level and greatest probability to succeed.

The smartest, most-skilled hunter is the trapper!

What is a trapper? A trapper is an animal that invests time and energy up-front using a systematic approach to hunting, which brings the prey to them. They never have to run or chase their prey, and they operate in complete silence at all times. Trappers never repel prey; instead, they attract it. They do not sit around and wait for things to happen; once they build their system, things automatically happen for them!

That is the highest and most effective skill in hunting.

You are going to be a trapper, but in our case, in business, you will be a benevolent trapper. You will be someone who builds a proven system that will keep a constant stream of massive revenue flowing indefinitely, while also delivering the highest level of integrity to your clients. Your output will multiply far beyond the up-front investment of time and energy you put in. Remember, it is all about having a system!

Once you properly create, implement, and maintain your system, you will never become a desperate predator, as described above. This is because, like the trapper, your system will work for you and not vice-versa. As a result, you will find that time is your most valuable resource.

Another way to make sure you set yourself apart from the negative perception of the predator and ensure your success, is to make it your primary goal to do things that are good for humanity. Setting this goal and operating your business under this principle will, in turn, be good for you and those around you. We have achieved immense success by applying this simple principle to our business, and if you follow it, you will too. We will discuss what we call The Give Back Strategy, in-depth later.

The primary rule of any great business model is that the client always wins first. When the client wins first, you are a real influencer. You get someone to agree or buy, and his or her life is made better by that decision. They will be grateful to you for what you have done for them.

Why make that obvious distinction? Here's why.

A win/win is when the client and the business both benefit from an encounter.

When the business wins, but the client feels manipulated, that is a win/lose outcome. If the client doesn't feel they are winning in the transaction, that is a loss for you. It would be best if you always were thinking about and trying to create win/win situations for both you and your client. That's the big difference between a trapper and a predator!

Trappers influence and predators manipulate.

Now we will drop a bit of a bomb; the skills used to acquire the client may be the same for both the trapper and the predator. Both can be very good at what they do.

The glaring difference between the two is their intentions and, therefore, the outcomes they produce. Read that again, because if you are going to create sustainable wealth, you need to fully comprehend the difference between influence and manipulation.

Believe it or not, manipulation is not the worst thing that can happen in business. As terrible as it is, there is something far worse.

The worst thing that can happen in business is that you have an idea, product, service, or an opportunity that you know will benefit a potential client. You know it, and even they know it, but you cannot get them there. They tell you "no" because, for some reason, you are repelling them instead of attracting them. Somehow, something you are doing is causing their defenses to rise unnecessarily. Something must be wrong with your approach. You are not a manipulator because your intentions are good, but you have created a lose/lose scenario, nonetheless. Lose/lose is the worst outcome, as we stated above. The client loses because their life is not made better by buying, and you lose because you cannot monetize on an event that should have been a no-brainer. Our intention for this book is to turn lose/lose into win/win for you and your clients!

With all that said, you must understand that to be a benevolent trapper and a multi-millionaire, you need to be in business for yourself. Notice that we said, "for yourself," not "by yourself." With our system, you are going to learn the skills required to get everyone around you to help you build a successful business!

This does not mean you cut and run from the job that is currently paying your bills, or the career for which you trained. It does mean you need to begin building the mindset of a business owner, and if you have not already done so, take concrete steps towards starting that business.

Let's address what the term "business" conjures in the mind of a potential entrepreneur. When people see the word "business," they often think of a business as a "brick and mortar" office or storefront with significant overhead, inventory, and employees; requiring multiple licenses and permits.

This misconception is one of the more perilous falsehoods that influence what people think it means to be a business owner. The point is, if you think that starting a business is daunting, we are here to tell you it does not have to be.

The majority of people who have gotten rich following our system started with minimal investment, no inventory, office space, equipment, or even employees!

Most even stayed at their current jobs until they were able to replace their income, something they were able to achieve remarkably fast. Furthermore, many of these same people were able to generate annual cash flow in the six and seven figures before even contemplating opening an actual brick and mortar office.

Do you want to know a secret? Many of these people still do not have a physical office. Their ability to earn a high residual income so quickly made a physical office, and the overhead that accompanies it, unnecessary!

Instead, they have a system for success that creates endless residual income, forever, from which all the gold flows. Before you learn the system in this book, it is vital to understand how any business of substance is born. All businesses start with a need. You are not required to come up with a novel or unique need that has not been satisfied; you can jump into any business where there is an established need and flourish!

In Terry and Don's case, success came from jumping into the insurance business, a business that had already been around for hundreds of years! They certainly didn't create the need for insurance on their own. What they did was, find unique ways to approach the insurance business, which led to their incredible success. You can do this too.

That unique approach is what we are here to teach you. By now, you should understand that there is a system to succeed in any endeavor. If you do, then you are considerably ahead of the crowd who sits around and wonders what is happening (like the scavenger) - instead of making things happen (like the trapper)!

Even if you do not embrace all of the methods that we present to you in this book, just recognizing that success is built from systems, is a true revelation! Remember, all of nature runs on systems - the human body runs on integrated systems working together. The entire universe itself is an infinite set of systems that have been running seamlessly for billions of years!

IMPORTANT: The simplest system for success in business can be summarized as follows:

- Identify a problem. (This is your business).

- Find a remedy or solution to that problem. (This is your product or service).

- Find people with that problem. (Your "stocked lake" from which to fish).

- Get them to meet with you. (The marketing system we will teach you).

- Get them to bring perpetual new customers to you free of charge! (OUR GOLD MINE SYSTEM!!).

- Duplicate your business model. (Creating leverage and perpetual residual income).

If you are reading this and saying to yourself, "No kidding, I know this is how people get rich," the question we have for you is, what is taking you so long to achieve success then? Why haven't **you** materialized massive success yourself? It's OK; we have the answers to these questions, you don't have to worry. You, too, are experiencing what we also experienced in the past until we cracked the code. We wrote this book to share these insights with you.

This book is not meant to push you into starting your own business. You have likely already been considering that, or otherwise, you would not be seeking the kinds of answers this book will provide.

We designed this book to give you a detailed blueprint on how to set up, run, and maintain a successful system in your business. If you follow the plan we have laid out for you, you can find the success you are seeking and build wealth faster than you ever imagined.

Terry and Don want to make sure you are still with them, as the next sentence is critical to understand before we go any further.

They do not make cold calls!

My friends, to be perfectly clear, they hate cold calling as much, if not more than you do! They would never even consider building a business that requires constant cold calls. In their many years of combined experience, any business built on cold calls is inefficient, unsustainable, and therefore bound to fail. Instead, they developed a system. A system from which, once you learn and implement into your business, you will receive constant and perpetual benefits immediately - as they did and continue to receive.

After a few hours of running our system, you will never have to cold call again! You read that correctly; we said within a few hours, not years, months, weeks, or even days. Hours! Soon you will see for yourself how this is possible.

Though we have yet to unveil our system to you, let's say for argument's sake, that our statement about you never having to cold call again is true. How easy would it be for you to build wealth and leverage if you did not have to cold call and were still successful? Very easy, right?

Most people will never admit this, but a primary reason why many people do not go into sales or fail in their own business is their fear of cold calling. People inherently dread talking to strangers, even if what they are offering is of great benefit to that person.

The fear of cold calling is the unspoken Achilles' heel that inhibits growth - and as stated above, most people will never even admit to having this fear. Who wants to admit they are afraid to do something so simple? Cold calling is merely talking to strangers, perhaps asking for an appointment to view a product or service that could potentially improve their lives. Rest assured, we, too, can relate to this fear. After all, from birth, we've been taught by our parents not to talk to strangers! Stranger danger, right?

Instead of admitting this fear surrounding cold calls, people will give a plethora of excuses to avoid them. Such as: "It's a bad product," "No need," "Bad management," "Unfair pricing by competition," "Bad compensation model," "Poor leads," etc. Anything to avoid making those calls!

Well, two successful entrepreneurs who have built amazing systems for success are admitting to all who read this book: they hate cold calling too!

Do you know who else hates cold calls? People who would otherwise be your client or customer, had you approached them by **any** method other than a cold call.

As a general rule, and as stated above, people tend to reject the concept of cold calls, even if they would positively benefit from the product, service, or idea presented to them during the call! We all are **naturally** prone to get defensive in the presence of "salespeople," which is understandable.

Remember, the hunters that make noise and repel their prey - well guess what, cold calling is very "noisy"!

As a rule of thumb, humans get defensive when they are involved in a situation that works against their natural processes for wanting or needing something. Sales and cold calling, when done improperly, raise those defenses. It is for this reason that the "sales" profession has such bad connotations associated with it.

You will not be someone who works against human nature; instead, you will master techniques to become someone whose mere presence does not raise defenses in potential clients. Your approach will work calmly, clearly, and in harmony with your client, which will attract them to you. Once you have built a solid professional relationship based on trust and transparency with your clients, they will invite you into their social circle of friends and family. Your objective will be to learn to make the sales process **natural!**

You will be the benevolent trapper! You are going to do it right and receive handsome rewards as a result!

Please remember, despite these negative connotations mentioned above, sales is continually the highest paid profession.

Chapter Three

The Painful Truth a.k.a. The "You're probably not going to like this, but it needs to be said if you want the life of your dreams," discussion.

In this next chapter, we will address one of the greatest lies ever told about business and success. Although this chapter's title says it all, we cannot move forward with introducing you to our system until we deal with and expose this lie. Too often, we have heard people say that the fastest way to success is to turn your passion or hobby into a revenue-generating business.

WARNING: *This is a blatant falsehood. It could not be further from the truth.*

We could include several hundred extra pages of data and examples of cases where this "truism" has been proven wrong time and again, but we will cut to the chase instead and steer you in the right direction. Anecdotally, there are stories in the news about people who have turned their hobbies into successful businesses. However, think about how you learned about these stories... from the darn news!

What does that mean? The news deals in rarities and sensationalism, not in stories that are common occurrences or the norm. Simply put, these stories are anomalies. They can mislead us into thinking that passion is the primary ingredient for success. What are the essential ingredients for success? Drive, absolutely! Passion, not so much. Neither Terry nor Don started in life with a passion for selling insurance. What they did have was an incredible drive and an unwillingness to fail. Most successful people, truly wealthy people, become wealthy from a viable business and rarely by monetizing their hobby!

To further demonstrate this point, let's look at the example of a teacher who is also a talented baker. She not only loves to bake, but she receives constant compliments and reinforcement from her friends and family for her baking skills.

In fact, in passing, several of them have said that she should open a bakery!

(Don't do it, Ms. Teacher!)

The teacher decides to take a loan from her only retirement account, quits her teaching job, and opens a bakery.

Would you like to finish the story, or shall we? You guessed it. Sadly, within 12-24 months of opening the bakery, the teacher is broke, jobless, and in debt. What's even worse, she now hates her once-beloved passion for baking!

Everyone reading this book knows at least one person who has fallen into this same trap. It is a cautionary tale.

Our next example is of an artist who has a passion for painting. The only problem is that he is a terrible painter. His friends and family keep telling him to "keep at it" and "follow his passion," and everything will "work out." Unfortunately, more often than not, things don't just "work out." We are not saying this to be negative; we are just trying to be realistic and painting the picture as it is, not as we merely wish it to be. *(Painting pun intended)*.

It bears mentioning that there is nothing malicious about your family and friends believing in you and encouraging you to pursue a career you love. But that alone is not enough. As we know, our loved ones tend to see only the best in us and are not always the most honest and forthright when it comes to matters of skill. **Especially** if it is a skill for which we have expressed an interest and a desire to pursue. No one wants to be responsible for "crushing someone else's dreams," so to speak. But all of this is a crutch. We are doing more harm than good by not being honest with those we love.

What about professional athletes? They indeed have turned their hobbies or passions as youths into lucrative businesses. First, most Division 1 college-level athletes never make it to the professional ranks. That is a fact. Yes, some of these athletes that reach the professional ranks can make a lot of money, but the ride typically only lasts for a short amount of time.

Although professional athletes get to enjoy playing a sport for a living, ask any professional athlete how closely they follow that sport after they retire. Unless they move into broadcasting or coaching, virtually no ex-professional athletes continue to engage in their sport after they no longer play. Many end up resenting their sport and all it represents. Remember, these athletes are just employees working for large organizations. Very few can leverage assets of the team owners and the leagues who employ them. They had no ownership – no skin in the game.

Terry is a perfect example of an athlete who continues to enjoy his hobby well into adulthood, while making money to support this hobby **but** without relying on his passion to generate income. Terry is a world-ranked amateur motocross racer. It's one of his many passions and hobbies. Could he be a top professional in his class? Sure, but at what price? He would be in constant competition to maintain his world ranking, against an ever-increasing group of younger riders.

Much like the predator that we discussed in chapter two, with any professional physical sport, the skills required to be at the top of one's game diminish over time. To stay at the top of his sport as a professional athlete, Terry would need to work and train harder for equal or less money. Working in this manner is the opposite of what it means to have leverage and freedom. Eventually, Terry, like most professional athletes, would come to resent the sport that was once his passion.

Instead, Terry makes millions as an investor and business owner. Thanks to his financial success, he can ride and compete at the highest amateur levels, doing so with the best motocross bikes, equipment, and support available. He enjoys all the luxuries and benefits of a top professional, with none of the drawbacks. This is all because he decided to keep his passion and business separate and learned to use one to feed the other. As a result, he rides and races when he wants, on his terms, securing his love of the sport for years to come - win/win.

Look, we are not telling you all this to kill your dreams; instead, we are trying to ensure that they come true! We want you to create and maintain a lifetime of residual income so that you can pursue your passions and hobbies on your time!

The fact is you need to start a business that allows you to make a significant amount of money, which gives you leverage, freedom, and a lifetime of residual income!

Do you know what is always true? When you make a lot of money, you tend to enjoy your business more. Although this may sound obvious, we want you to understand the path to happiness in today's world is paved with leveraged income, which will allow you to create the freedom you are seeking.

So, if you really want to live your passions and enjoy your hobbies, you need to figure out a way to make this happen without ever having to worry about earning a living doing it.

Chapter Four

The Trinity of Success

Our favorite acronym is S.Y.S.T.E.M.: **S**aving **Y**ou **S**tress, **T**ime, **E**nergy, and **M**oney.

Be a trapper, remember?

We encourage you to embrace the concept that without a system, there is no path to success. In fact, in order to perfect our system, you will need to combine three systems, working together, to become successful as an entrepreneur and become a wealthy business professional.

These three systems are identified in this book as the "Trinity of Success."

They are:

1. Giving

2. Your Word

3. Movement and Momentum

We know you are familiar with the standard definition of these words, but how they apply to our system, as we will show you, are **nothing short of miraculous.**

Giving

In the next few chapters, we develop the system of giving. We call it *The Give Back Strategy*. The concept is to allow the natural giving process to unfold between you and the client.

Here, you will begin the process of building your business to receive continuous help from your clients, friends, and family. Not only will you learn the skill of asking for help, but you will also do so in a way that makes your clients, friends, and family more than eager to assist you!

Your Word

In chapter seven, you will learn perhaps the greatest sales method known to humankind! We will teach you how to close business with confidence and use our closing strategy to generate perpetual referrals.

The best part of using our method is that it ensures you maintain the utmost level of integrity between both you and the client, by using the power of your word as a bond.

Remember we said by using our system you will never need to cold call again? In chapter seven, we will show you a method called *The Three Agreements*, where that promise becomes a reality!

Movement and Momentum

In chapter eight, we tie the anchor down with "BombShelly." BombShelly is the system that you will use to run your business!

It is nearly impossible to run a business without the system we are about to show you, yet most new business owners have nothing like it in place. As we have stated countless times thus far, running a business without the proper systems in place such as BombShelly, is a deal killer, but that gets fixed today!

The power you will possess when the three systems are working together is unstoppable!

At first, it may seem overwhelming to have three systems running at once, but all three are designed to work together, intuitively, to create massive success. However, if you were to integrate only one of the systems into your success plan, you would still be miles ahead of most.

Once you begin to develop, build, and implement your Trinity of Success, not only will you be amazed by its simplicity, you will quickly see the power it wields from its immediate results.

What we tend to see is certain successful people climb the ladder and then kick it down to make it more difficult for others to achieve the same level of success after them. The textbook definition of a "scarcity" mentality is the myth that there is only so much finite wealth, and a limited number of people that may achieve that wealth. These "manipulators" want you to believe that the success they have achieved is not obtainable for you because there is not enough to go around.

Do not believe this propaganda!

Those who perpetuate the falsehood that success is difficult to achieve, often feel guilty when they become wealthy, attributing their success to luck or chance. They feel that they do not deserve success because they didn't work as hard as they thought that they needed to achieve the level of success attained.

What is more likely is that success was not as unachievable as they were led to believe it should be in the first place!

While this may be the case for some, it is not the standard for the millions who experience great success today. To ensure you do not believe achieving success is due to luck or chance, the system you build will produce unequivocal evidence that your success is due entirely to you. Not only will you see the return on your efforts, but you will also be able to help others duplicate the same success for themselves.

It is critical to keep in mind that the universe has an infinite amount of resources. Although you may know this instinctually, continually hearing people tell you that something "cannot be done" or how "extremely difficult" it is to achieve success, starts to affect one's psyche. The infiltration of this uncertainty may ultimately affect your trust in yourself as well. You begin to believe things which you know are not true! Don't allow this to happen!

This is an excellent segue to the next point we want to emphasize; success does not need to be difficult, but it does require you to work hard and work smart.

Generally speaking, people get confused between the terms "difficult work" and "hard work." When things are deemed difficult, it may cause us to struggle. As a result, we tend to shut down and are more likely to give up and quit, which is a natural response.

What we have seen time and again, is that people are willing to work hard once they know exactly what they are supposed to do. The "not knowing" is what makes achieving success seem difficult. As the old saying goes, "Knowledge is power!"

What you will read in the following chapters will prove to you that not only is it possible to achieve great success regardless of what you may believe or have been told, it is also not difficult. However, as we have stressed to you, becoming a success does require hard work, intention, and smart thinking.

Remember, the trappers dedicate all of their energy, investment, and hard work up-front, to build a system that brings success to them. They do this by attracting their prey instead of wasting resources chasing after it.

By implementing your system over a set period of time, you will create a vacuum filled with clients, money, and opportunities, which all lead to success! While this may not happen overnight, it should not take months, or even years to achieve when done correctly.

Some information provided in this book might be new to you, so don't expect to grasp everything all at once. Although these concepts are *simple* to understand, they are by no means *easy*. Take your time and be patient with yourself. Don't be afraid to go back at your own pace and review all the systems we lay out for you. There is no rush. We highly recommend that you read these next chapters several times and take detailed notes as you read through the book and underline key concepts to revisit.

The next crucial step is to start building the most sacred place to develop your business: your war room. A war room is a physical space in your home or office, where you can plan, write on whiteboards, brainstorm, think, and create. Make room to put up charts on the walls so you can see the tangible effects of your business growing!

The final important step in preparing yourself to get started, is to let go of whatever part of your thought process has not been serving you up to this point. We speak at length in our workshops and training events about how to get out of our own way. We know it is not easy, but here and now is where you do that. Replace these old ideas and ways of thinking with the new outlook and game plan, which we provide for you within these pages.

Make sure you enlist and demand the support of your family throughout this process. They are integral to your success. It is a mystery as to why family always seems willing to "support" our failures but tend to be wary of celebrating our accomplishments. Let them know that you need 100% of their support with your new endeavor.

Now is the time to begin building your first system!

An old Chinese proverb states, "The best time to plant a tree was 20 years ago. The second best time is now."

Forget about 20 years ago; now is your time.

Chapter Five

The S.Y.S.T.E.M. - Part One
The Big Give Back Secret a.k.a. the Greatest Chapter in the History of Books

You might be thinking to yourself that the title of this chapter is a very bold statement. *The greatest chapter in the history of books;* it is indeed, and soon, you will agree.

Typically, in other books of this kind, a statement like the one we have just made is hidden deep inside 20 chapters of drivel as the author drags on and on, often never quite revealing what actually made them a success. The few authors, who do reveal how they achieved their success, tend not to break it down into simple and cohesive concepts, such as **S.Y.S.T.E.M.**, which can be duplicated by others. We will do the opposite and break our systems down for you step-by-step, in a clear, easy-to-follow, and comprehensible manner.

Within these pages, we will show you the foundational S.Y.S.T.E.M. that all dynamic client-based businesses are built upon, and which have worked for decades. The only issue is that no one seems to be teaching it properly anymore.

The first concept of The Trinity of Success is *The Give Back Strategy*. *The Give Back Strategy* is what undoubtedly led to Terry and Don's success. Although they utilized it for years, the secret was never articulated until recently when they finally recognized it for what it was - a cohesive system.

In addition to highlighting the reasons why many people who become entrepreneurs subsequently fail, *The Give Back Strategy* also exposes one of the most significant shortcomings in business. We will cover that a bit later, but let's begin by taking a look at the simple script that Terry wrote several years ago on a cocktail napkin.

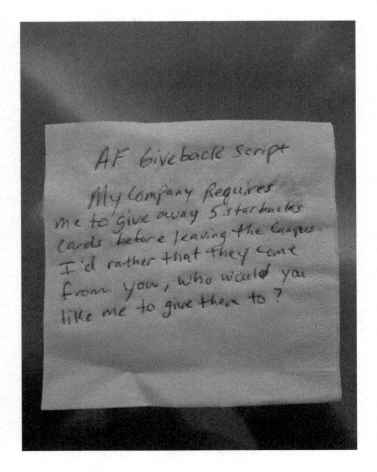

One might read the sentences written on this cocktail napkin and think, *"So what? It's just a simple referral script."*

My friends, anyone can make things complicated. As Steve Jobs said, "Simple can be harder than complex; You have to work hard to get your thinking clean to make it simple. But it's worth it in the end because once you get there, you can move mountains."

Chapter Five

The S.Y.S.T.E.M. - Part One
The Big Give Back Secret a.k.a. the Greatest Chapter in the History of Books

You might be thinking to yourself that the title of this chapter is a very bold statement. *The greatest chapter in the history of books;* it is indeed, and soon, you will agree.

Typically, in other books of this kind, a statement like the one we have just made is hidden deep inside 20 chapters of drivel as the author drags on and on, often never quite revealing what actually made them a success. The few authors, who do reveal how they achieved their success, tend not to break it down into simple and cohesive concepts, such as **S.Y.S.T.E.M.**, which can be duplicated by others. We will do the opposite and break our systems down for you step-by-step, in a clear, easy-to-follow, and comprehensible manner.

Within these pages, we will show you the foundational S.Y.S.T.E.M. that all dynamic client-based businesses are built upon, and which have worked for decades. The only issue is that no one seems to be teaching it properly anymore.

The first concept of The Trinity of Success is *The Give Back Strategy*. *The Give Back Strategy* is what undoubtedly led to Terry and Don's success. Although they utilized it for years, the secret was never articulated until recently when they finally recognized it for what it was - a cohesive system.

In addition to highlighting the reasons why many people who become entrepreneurs subsequently fail, *The Give Back Strategy* also exposes one of the most significant shortcomings in business. We will cover that a bit later, but let's begin by taking a look at the simple script that Terry wrote several years ago on a cocktail napkin.

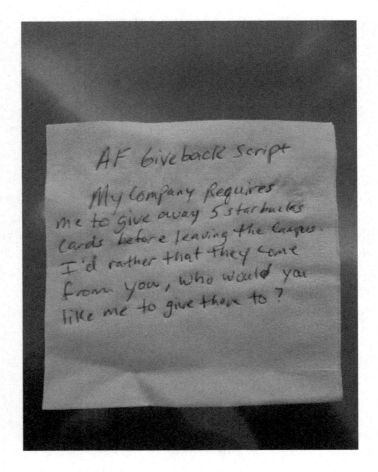

One might read the sentences written on this cocktail napkin and think, *"So what? It's just a simple referral script."*

My friends, anyone can make things complicated. As Steve Jobs said, "Simple can be harder than complex; You have to work hard to get your thinking clean to make it simple. But it's worth it in the end because once you get there, you can move mountains."

What Terry discovered, whether intentionally or unintentionally, is the power of *The Give Back Strategy*. Before we reveal its hidden treasures, however, let us back up and start by telling Terry's story.

Early in his career, Terry was struggling in his chosen field of financial services. He had a passion for finance, combined with a love for helping others. Unfortunately, and as we discussed in chapter three, passion alone is rarely, if ever, enough to achieve massive success. During this time, Terry made moderate sales but did not materialize the degree of wealth he desired and imagined for himself. Many of you reading this right now can probably identify with how Terry felt. Growing up in a family who owned a construction business, working hard was something to which Terry was accustomed. He knew how to work hard and was not afraid to do so. But, despite his hard work and devotion to his new career, he sensed that something was just not clicking.

Every day when he woke up, it seemed as though he had to start all over again, as if he had made no headway from the previous day. He operated almost robotically. Day after day, from one transaction to another, feeling as if he made little, if any, progress.

Financially, Terry's income climbed painfully slow. Each year the money he earned grew at a rate far lower than the financial expectations and goals he set for himself. Certainly, below what he knew he could achieve.

Looking back at this time, Terry sarcastically "brags" about doubling his income every year for three years, but before you scoff and call him a snob, understand that the progression looked like this:

Year one - $8,000

Year two - $16,000

Year three - $32,000

As you can see from the figures above, for those first three years while his income did, in fact, double every year, Terry was still not earning what is considered a living wage.

Given the time and energy he invested in his business, Terry did not see the kinds of returns he knew he could achieve. He was barely meeting his financial responsibilities and had no excess income for savings or additional investments for his and his family's future. He felt trapped.

At the end of the first three-year period of his new endeavor, Terry's family and friends pressured him to quit his failed venture and get a "real job." He had a wife and kids, bills, a mortgage, as well as many other responsibilities that were narrowly being met.

One morning, Terry had a terrifying realization while browsing the "jobs" section of the Sunday newspaper he was not even qualified for most of the available jobs he saw posted. He barely graduated high school with a 2.30 GPA, and only attended college for two months. Most of the job postings required a college degree and many years of experience. He thought to himself that if the only job he was qualified for was flipping burgers, he would rather live in a cardboard box!

This was a pivotal moment for Terry. He remembers reaching his lowest point shortly after this realization. Terry recalls collapsing on the floor in his closet, crying for hours, while contemplating his failure. We are sure many of you have found yourselves in similar moments, asking as Terry did, *"Why is it so difficult to achieve success?"* Remember our point earlier about difficult work versus hard work? Terry stood at the same crossroads that so many of you reading this book have already faced. He was looking for answers and guidance, sadly feeling there were none to be found.

At that moment, Terry did something that would change his life forever; **he made a full commitment to himself and decided that failure would no longer be an option. Quitting was off the table!**

(This is important for you to do as well!)

Then out of nowhere, as if the universe accepted Terry's commitment to success, a door suddenly opened for him. In this instance, he gained a new vision previously hidden from his view. Up until that that moment, Terry was trapped in the "scarcity" mentality, which left him feeling helpless, unable to attain the life he wanted for himself and his family.

The vision that Terry had that day is what this chapter is all about. His struggle and subsequent meteoric rise out of the "scarcity" mentality into abundance with an unwillingness to fail, will become the template for your plan of action that will lead you on your path to great success.

Soon after this pivotal moment, things changed quickly for Terry, and his sales started to skyrocket. While he attributed his recent increase in sales to his new outlook, he was still not at the level of success, and more importantly, income that he had desired. One momentous day in his office, his assistant said something that would soon revolutionize an entire industry! Seemingly out of the blue, she suggested that Terry go to the local elementary school and bring lunch to the staff.

Terry was perplexed. *"Bring the staff lunch?"* he thought. *"Why?"*

She went on to explain that she previously worked for a man whose business focused on helping teachers and public employees plan for their retirement.

She added that this man lived in a mansion in the hills of Southern California due to the success he achieved from this business.

Terry was understandably intrigued. Following his assistant's suggestion, he decided to take a plate of sandwiches to a local elementary school.

Although Terry had no idea what to expect next, he felt there was something to her suggestion. He just knew it. However, like a dog chasing a car, Terry had no idea what to do, had the driver stopped, and handed him the keys! He had to rely on trust.

To make a long story short, as a result of this simple action on that fateful day, Terry created what is now the number one 403(b) financial services agency in the United States. Today, his company has thousands of agents in over 50 major markets and has generated hundreds of millions of dollars in assets. By the simple act of giving to others, Terry created a specific and unique niche market that led to his extreme success.

For those of you who are not familiar with 403(b) plans, they are retirement accounts for public sector employees, much like a 401(k) plan is to the private sector. The successful business Terry created started from giving sandwiches to a group of hard-working, underserved, local elementary school teachers! Unbelievable, right? As outrageous as it might sound, this story is 100% true.

Terry had expected to set some appointments, give a bit of retirement advice, and move on. Terry did not expect, nor could he possibly have predicted, the reciprocity and appreciation he would receive from the teachers as a result. He found that the teachers were more than willing to give him referrals on the spot. Here is the key; they were willing to give him referrals without him even asking. The simple gesture of giving, even just a plate of sandwiches, opened up something in those teachers.

The fact that Terry committed never to quit, put him in the right mindset to be open to the suggestion from his assistant that launched an industry. Still, the help he was getting from his new clients was not prompted by him; it was given willingly by them. The problem was that Terry didn't know what to do with the help he received from the teachers. He went from one client to another, not fully aware of the powerful tool he created. Terry lacked intention. He did not realize the referral system was working because he was not aware that he was even **using** a system.

He soon realized he needed to fix this.

In building his business, Terry worked tirelessly to refine his sales processes. He needed to ensure that every move he made and the methods he was using were intentional. This was important because he wanted to hire and train other agents to join him in expanding his business into other territories as quickly as possible. This meant his system had to be easily taught and replicated by others to produce the same results every time.

Terry realized it was critical for his salespeople to become successful much faster than he did and to avoid the same setbacks he experienced along the way. He needed to duplicate his success, and quickly!

Early on his path to success, Terry noticed he was missing a specific and impactful way to meet new prospects. It was always something he found extremely difficult to do.

Terry thought asking his existing clients for referrals was uncomfortable and unnatural. He felt greedy, asking for more from his clients after he already made a sale. He felt this way even though he **knew** he was genuinely helping his clients to retire with dignity. Over time, he started to wonder that if his clients were benefiting from his services and products, then wouldn't his clients want their colleagues, friends, and families to have the same security? At this moment, Terry accepted that his mindset had to change because trying to find new prospects over and over each day was not sustainable.

Terry accepted that he needed to become a student (no pun intended) of his clients, the teachers. *"Why do people become teachers,"* he thought to himself? Certainly not to get rich, he realized. He began to study his clients over time and discovered their shared personality traits. Specifically, that teachers choose to educate children because they tend to be selfless and love to give back to others.

This is a good place for us to take a pause...

Before we go any further and get deeper into *The Give Back Strategy*, we need to expand your knowledge of the human brain, particularly the part of the brain that is affected by generosity and the act of giving.

Start by taking a look at yourself. If you are reading this book, we can already deduce certain things about you because not everyone is drawn to this kind of book. It tends to appeal to those who want to better themselves and help others. We can all agree that there is a definite "feel good" moment when you see the face of someone you are helping light up in acknowledgment of your generosity. This moment leads to what is often called the "giver's glow" or "helper's high."

Research shows the "feel good" effect is far from fleeting. Generosity positively affects our brains and our health, possibly even extending our lives. Simply put, being kind, generous, and caring for others is good for you too!

Professor Stephen Post is prolific on this subject and has researched and written on it at great length. His studies have continually found that generosity and compassion have been a focal point of research for decades. These studies consistently show that mood improvement, better physical health, and increased longevity of life directly connect to the act of giving - whether it's monetary donations or volunteer hours invested in others. When it comes to your health, it truly is better to give than to receive. According to Post, there were increased health benefits for those with chronic illness after giving to others. [1]

Post has stated that the feel-good effects of giving begin in the brain and may improve physical health and longevity because it helps to reduce stress. The giver's glow is a result of the transmission of several different happiness chemicals in the brain, including dopamine and endorphins, which give people a sense of euphoria. Euphoria is associated with tranquility, serenity, and inner peace. The pleasure and reward system has evolved, and at its most basic level, is tied to the joy we receive from eating, sex, and social interactions. Giving to others can even lower your blood pressure! [2]

Viewing the brain with MRI technology during moments of acts of generosity or selfless behavior has led scientists to uncover that even the thought of giving can trigger this innate response. [3]

Helping each other is equally healthy for all of us. As Mahatma Gandhi said, "The best way to find yourself is to lose yourself in the service of others."

Don talks about the giving concept as it applies to the subconscious mind in his book, "60-Seconds to Yes", in modules one through six on the online training platform (link provided later). Specifically, the process of giving is built into our natural survival mechanisms, substantiating how important it is to us! Our built-in survival mechanisms do not have time nor patience for peripheral efforts, unlike the mechanisms within the conscious mind. If something is in the subconscious mind, it means it is critical to human survival!

People feel good when they see the effects of the act of giving helping others. It can also inspire the receiver to give as a result.

The Proceedings of the National Academy of Science published a study showing that when one person behaves generously, it inspires observers to behave generously later, toward different people. The researchers even found that this altruism could be spread by three degrees beyond the original giver! [4]

Many studies attempting to explain the benefits of giving have consistently shown that giving makes people feel good and that selfless action can help lessen the risk and symptoms of depression or even everyday stress.

A study published in 2013 in the American Journal of Public Health, found that giving time and assistance to others reduced the mortality risk tied to stress, a known risk factor for many chronic diseases. According to the study, which looked at more than 800 adults in the Detroit area, stress did not predict mortality for participants who had helped others within the previous year. [5] But the link between stress and mortality was apparent in people **who did not** lend a helping hand, even after adjusting for age, health, and other variables.

Another study, published in the Journal of Health Psychology, followed more than 2,000 residents of Marin County, California, found that volunteerism reduced mortality rates more than exercising four times weekly and/or attending church regularly (another behavior tied to improved mental health and greater longevity). [6]

Subjects who volunteered for two or more causes had a 63 percent lower mortality rate than people who did not volunteer during the study period.

A 2008 study performed by a professor at Harvard Business School and his colleagues from another university, also found that people are happier when they spend money on others versus on themselves.

The study concluded that money actually does buy happiness, but not because people are spending it on themselves. Through human connections, money flows to both the giver and the receiver by creating a higher sense of well-being. [7]

Believe it or not, even thinking about giving money to a meaningful cause engages this evolutionary reward system, according to research led by Jorge Moll of the D'Or Institute for Research and Education in Brazil. [8]

However, there is one catch which we must mention - the giving must be heartfelt! Brain imaging has also shown that people experience even more brain activation when they give voluntarily. [9]

It is important to note what your intentions are and how you feel about the act of giving. For example, giving a meaningful donation can have a significant impact on the giver and the receiver. Just as important, if the act of giving is trivial or done begrudgingly, it will probably not have the same effect. Writing a check in hopes of lessening your stress without thought as to where the money is going, would likely not be as beneficial as giving from the heart to a charity that personally touches you.

Whether you are giving time, money, or a helping hand to others, you stand to receive the stress-busting advantages of altruism. Giving in a meaningful way, or even contemplating such heartfelt generosity, takes the focus off yourself and the things that may weigh you down.

When you are able to give in a selfless manner, you will find this all comes very easily, and the potential windfall can be significant. Giving in the presence of the benefactor, has the maximum benefit to you, creating the 'giver's glow' we mentioned earlier. Again, consider what you know about yourself; when giving selflessly, without the expectation of receiving anything in return, your friendships are deeper, you are more likely to sleep better, and you can handle life's obstacles with greater ease.

Now let's get back to Terry's story. What he discovered the day he handed out the sandwiches is the gift he gave his clients by merely asking for their help! What he found was that his clients were more than eager to help him with the gift of referrals! **Bear in mind, this was not for the express interest of helping Terry alone, but for the benefits and rewards they received in return from giving! The teachers experienced the giver's glow by giving Terry referrals.**

Considering how giving works in the brain, for Terry not to ask for help in building his business would be depriving those who he cares for the opportunity to care for others. Over time, he began to view these referrals as "gifts," which allowed others to experience the giver's glow. Allowing his clients to provide these "gifts" of referrals became the only way Terry would operate his business moving forward.

The indisputable and invaluable lesson Terry learned is that **it takes the help of others to grow a business**. At the same time, he established a viable and scalable system, which provided measurable results and could be easily taught to others.

This concept is so simple and effective that it can be applied to any business. Contrary to what you may have heard, there is no such thing as a self-made millionaire. The problem has always been the perception and stigma of shame that we wrongfully attach to asking others for help.

We all have fears, hesitations, pride, all of which can inhibit our ability to ask others for help. However, as mentioned above, it would be selfish to deny others of the pure joy they receive from helping you as well. Remember, this means any form of help, no matter how large or small, it is always important to reach out to others for help in growing your business. Don't be afraid to ask for help; you have nothing to lose and everything to gain.

Take a minute to look at your own business. Whether it is already up and running or you are just getting started, it needs a foundational building block. That building block, from a sales perspective, is simple; you must create a referral-based business!

When done correctly, referrals are the simplest, least expensive, and most powerful form of marketing!

When executed properly, referrals are received in a low-defense manner, such that people are grateful to you for asking to assist those closest to them!

We also strongly believe in personal contact, i.e., meeting knee-to-knee with the client. Hiding behind "noisy" gimmicks will most likely result in loss of time, money, and cause unnecessary frustration for both you and your client. Instead of using these inefficient tactics, you will build a multi-pronged approach to your business where you will quickly see the benefits and rewards of developing a powerful referral strategy. Using our system will help you achieve the success you desire much faster.

Remember, we are in our own heads when it comes to the fear of asking others for referrals. You must face the age-old problem of fear and shame head-on. *"Will it cost me the sale?"* *"Am I worthy?"* We are here to tell you it won't cost you the sale and yes, of course, you are worthy!

Never in the history of our business, which is currently over 100,000 clients strong and growing every day, has a client EVER backed out of a deal, because we asked for a referral. We repeat; never, ever, ever has it happened.

Remember the blackjack game where there was zero risk of losing any money? This is what we are talking about; there are zero risks in asking for help!

Contrary to what you have been told or you may believe, nothing is 100% certain, in business or in life, except RIGHT HERE! It's 100% certain because giving to others will always come back to you - it is a universal law. At every one of the thousands of trainings Terry and Don have conducted over the past decade, involving thousands of sales professionals in various industries, they ask the question if anyone has ever lost a sale because they asked for a referral. Never has a single person raised their hand. Conversely, people have said they lost a sale by not asking for a referral because the prospect questioned the salesperson's belief in their own product or service!

You are guaranteed not to lose business by asking for help. In fact, you have a **moral obligation** to ask people for help to grow your business with referrals. People love to help each other. It is hardwired into their brains and makes them feel good.

Whether you are recruiting others to join your business, selling physical products, or providing services, you must ask yourself if you are maximizing and leveraging your clients as your number one growth source. In the next chapters, we are going to blow your minds with simple strategies that will get you over your fears and hesitations about asking for referrals.

We said this is the greatest chapter in the history of books. In case it isn't crystal clear so far, we will summarize it for you. You probably did not know prior to reading this chapter that asking for help has health benefits for both the giver and the receiver. Embrace this universal law, and it will change your life for the better!

Before we move on, we have a few questions that we would like you to ask yourself:

1) Do you believe in your business?

2) Do you believe what you do helps others?

3) Is the world a better place when people say "yes" to you?

If your answer is "yes" to any or all of these questions, you are ready to achieve massive success by building your first system with our simple-yet-powerful strategies!

Buckle up because the next chapter will not only expand your mind, it will fill your calendar and wallet!

Chapter Six

Giving and The Give Back Strategy

In this chapter, we are going to give you concrete strategies for building a thriving referral-based business. The purpose is clear; to create massive action that brings infinite prospects to you and your business, perpetually. First, we'll prime the pump to create a consistent flow of new customers to your venture.

Let's review the cocktail napkin with Terry's simple, yet effective, Give Back script. It is this script that he considers his game-changer.

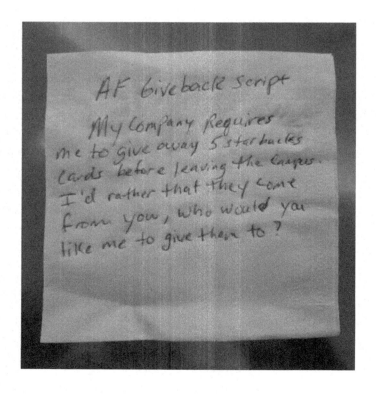

Terry's script is meant to be a reference, as we know yours will look different.

It has been mentioned more than once that simplicity is the foundation of any successful system.

To create a basic referral strategy, you must first compose a script. Once you have written a script and are satisfied with its contents and message, you need to practice it hundreds of times. We are not exaggerating; you need to practice the script hundreds of times. You must know the script so well that it becomes second nature to you, like your phone number or date of birth. Furthermore, it is only through practice and repetition that you will learn to sound natural and genuine when delivering the script to your audience. For the script to be effective, your audience must believe that you believe what you're telling them; otherwise, they won't! **WE REPEAT**: if you do not believe in the companies, products, opportunities, or services you are presenting, no one else will, regardless of how much you practice your script.

It is essential to discuss the core concept of giving back early in the script. Within the first sentence of Terry's script, you will notice that he makes the statement about giving back. It reads, *"My Company requires me to give away 5 Starbucks cards before leaving the campus..."* The next thing we must keep in mind is that the key to a successful script is keeping it short. A script, when written and delivered correctly, should be under 10 seconds. This may sound short, but we are only referring to the Give Back part of the script.

Also, when you're presenting to your audience, your script must flow without stopping to ask high-defense questions in the middle. Asking questions can distract your listener and cause them to lose focus. Losing focus = losing the sale!

We know that it is hard for a salesperson not to sound "salesy" when asking a potential client questions. We also know that sounding "salesy" will immediately raise the defenses. An example could be if a salesperson asks you, "You certainly don't like to waste money, do you?" Naturally, this would trigger your defenses to rise when a stranger asks such a personal and pointed question. Stay on track and to the point. If you go back and reread Terry's script, you will notice it flows all the way through in one breath to the **call-to-action**: in this case, asking for referrals. The call-to-action is the cue that we give the audience to let them know that we have finished our presentation, and now we expect something from them.

Notice that in Terry's script, there is no mention of asking the audience for permission to deliver the script. He gets straight to the point and gives the listener the exact amount of information he needs them to hear. He does not ask rhetorical questions like, "Wouldn't you like to help others here at the school?" Again, it is important to go directly to the call-to-action without veering off course. The more time we waste with chitchat or unnecessary information, the more "salesy" we may sound, and the less likely we are to keep the attention of our audience. We need to be mindful of peoples' time and maximize their attention, allowing them to focus on our message.

Side note: This is also how you ask for an appointment with a prospective client, whether on the phone, in person, or in an email. We suggest you use the same technique with a simple script that contains the call-to-action at the end. The call-to-action is not closed-ended, i.e., a "yes" or "no" question. It is always open-ended, "who," "what," "when," or "where?" Always close with an open-ended call-to-action. This is an important rule to keep in mind in any sales situation. By closing with a call-to-action, you essentially shortcut the path to getting a "yes," while not providing the prospect or client with an out.

The call-to-action makes the job easier for the person you are speaking with, as they want to be given instruction and guidance on what to do next. It is also important to never assume the client knows what you want or what you need from them. By establishing *The Give Back Strategy* at the very beginning of your script, you will seem non-threatening and will, therefore, elicit a low level of defense in your audience. Notice that Terry does not directly ask for referrals, but **rather frames the concept for the audience as their ability to give back to others.**

This is the core principle and purpose of *The Give Back Strategy*. Instead of asking our potential clients to give something to us, we are presenting an opportunity for them to give something to someone else. Listen carefully: this is a major shift in approach to the conventional sales pitch. Instead of making the prospects feel as though they are having something taken from them, it allows them to feel as though they can give. Remember from the previous chapter, how rewarding the giving feeling is for our brains and our overall well-being?

We know that the word "referral" in a sales setting can raise defenses and create a feeling of uneasiness within us all. It gives people a sense of being put on the spot and can cause them to shut down, and we can all identify with this feeling. For this reason, presenting something like a $5 gift card to Starbucks puts people at ease because we are introducing a gift, while simultaneously asking for help.

The principles and techniques we are presenting to you are effective because of basic human psychology. You don't need to be an expert in this field to understand these concepts, as they are mostly common sense and speak to human nature. We can all relate to these simple needs. Do not get confused; our goal is not to use our clients' needs to trick them or to take advantage of them. Instead, your ultimate goal is to create a harmonious ecosystem with your client of giving back that is mutually beneficial. You can only accomplish this goal if you know your client and knowing your client is about understanding their needs.

You must learn to incorporate these techniques in your approach, because knowing their needs will allow you to satisfy their needs.

Because of the school business model, Terry's future potential clients were often in the classroom right next door. That might not be the case for you in your business, but that is OK. Referrals can be contacted via telephone or email just as easily.

Below you will find the five steps to *The Give Back Strategy*, as well as a sample script to get an idea of how it works in a practical scenario.

As we mentioned before, *The Give Back Strategy* script is the first step in creating a much larger system. Here is the system we designed for the financial agents in our organization:

Step one: Meet with a teacher.

Step two: Deliver the Give Back script.

Step three: Finish meeting with the teacher and set the next appointment.

Step four: Go and see the first or closest teacher they referred to you.

Step five: Apply the referral script!

Here is an example of one of our agent's scripts:

AGENT:

"Hi there, Mrs. Jones, your friend Mary, next door, asked me to drop by and give you this gift card. (Agent hands Mrs. Jones the card). She thought you might be interested in what we are doing together, which is reviewing her retirement options. We will be here again tomorrow, what is a good time to meet for 10-15 minutes, after school or during your prep period?"

Let's pause here and break down what just took place between the agent and their potential client, Mrs. Jones.

First, to establish credibility with Mrs. Jones, the agent uses Mary's name at the beginning of the script. What the agent is **not** doing is wasting time with obligatory pleasantries such as, "How's your day going?" or "Isn't the weather great?" We highly recommend that you refrain from this kind of banter, as it is never perceived as genuine; get to the point.

Next, the agent gives Mary, her friend, credit for the gift card he is offering to Mrs. Jones. It is essential to always give credit to the person who referred you, the real hero.

Now understand the purpose of the gift card. (**Warning:** this next part will have some legalese, please bear with us). Based on the dollar amount we use, it is not considered a bribe or a quid pro quo.

What the "gift" really does is **provide 20 seconds of civility with a stranger right off the bat**. The person you are speaking to for those 20 seconds is listening to whatever comes out of your mouth next, so make it count. That is the true purpose of this small gift. It does not guarantee an appointment, nor are we holding the gift hostage in exchange for one.

We want to mention that it is essential for you to become familiar with the federal and state insurance laws as well as regulations regarding gifting versus rebating in the territories where you work. It is important that the "gift" be nominal as a token and is not meant to be part of a "bargained-for-exchange."

Please do your homework and due diligence to find out what the exact laws are regarding the legal amounts for a "gift" as it is crucial to operate your business with honesty and integrity and follow all state and federal laws. Within our company, we place due diligence, compliance, and transparency at the top of our priority list. We suggest you make these a priority for your businesses as well.

Phew, that part is over.

Finally, it is important to note that we hand the card to the person first before delivering the script. Twenty seconds of civility is all you need to get the next line out.

Again, by eliminating the small talk, we can get right to the call-to-action in one breath. Remember, we only have 10-15 seconds - wow, this method is brilliant. By following this technique, we are explaining the purpose of the meeting and what they can expect in terms of their time, i.e., 10-15 minutes of their day for the appointment. While we may need more time once the meeting starts, we never violate our initial promise regarding how much of their time the meeting will take. If we speak for 15 minutes and have not yet finished, we ask for permission to continue or ask if we can schedule a follow-up appointment. It is crucial to be mindful of their time and this is a rule to which you should strictly adhere. By honoring your promise and keeping the meeting within the promised timeframe, the potential client will appreciate the respect you showed for their time.

Never violate their trust by breaking your word. Ever!

Once the meeting is over, guess what we do? Yes, that is right, we deliver The Give Back script! At this point, the referral has been given the gift, and now it is their turn to feel the joy and euphoria of giving back. They have not heard the script yet, but they have seen its benefits. Because we did our job right and conducted ourselves with integrity, they are more than willing to give back to us with referrals.

We are creating a vortex for a win/win!

Now, you are starting to see how the system works. Lather, rinse, and repeat. While the content and details of your system may differ from ours depending on your business, you will have the same ability to build your own lather, rinse, and repeat system for success, as we did. The best part is that it can be tailor-made for any business!

The key is the call-to-action. By following this simple system, you make it easy for your potential clients, your team, and yourself. As you build your referral system, run it by others to check for high-defense words and actions that might turn off your audience. Brett Moore, one of our top business builders out of San Diego, has a favorite saying when training his new agents:

"Don't Be Weird!" or "DBW" as we have affectionately come to call it.

This should become the mantra for anyone building a sustainable business. The idea is to constantly improve, adjust, and refine your system. Successful trappers are always trying to improve their skills and become as efficient as possible with their system. It's an ongoing process, but it's what will make you successful. Remember, work hard and work smart.

On the next page is a diagram which illustrates the step-by-step structure of any successful referral system:

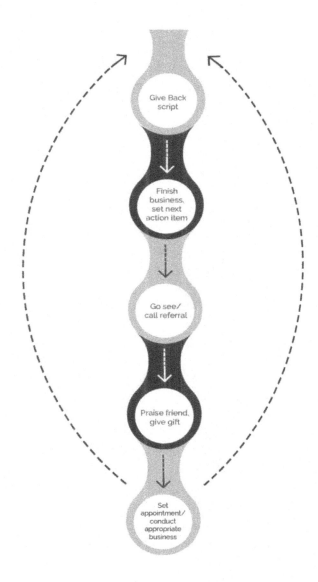

Lather, rinse, and repeat! There is nothing complicated about it.

Throughout this book, you will notice we use a sample script from our niche industry. When building your Give Back script, it does not necessarily need to involve giving a gift. A gift card works well in our business because the referrals are often located in the same building. You can still create *The Give Back Strategy* without a gift! The point is to find something that you can give back to your prospects in return for their referrals that they can then give to someone else. Remember, 'giver's glow'!

IMPORTANT: The following is a crucial component of *The Give Back Strategy*. When you get an appointment from the referral, you must immediately run back to the person who gave you the referral and tell them the good news! This also applies to any business you receive from that referral. These people want to know how things turned out!

It is vital to cultivate the giving mentality you initiated in the referrer. That person may have forgotten about the referrals they gave you, but they will be pleased to know the results of their efforts. It completes the loop of the giver's glow, and often leads to more referrals! As stated above, it is of the utmost importance to go back to the person that referred you and tell them the good news.

During our sales and business trainings, the question always comes up, *"When should I ask for referrals?"* The answer is simple - **often, and always**. When you first meet with someone, deliver *The Give Back Strategy* script. You will not lose business. The worst-case scenario is that you break even. They may tell you that they want to see what you can do for them first. Folks, that is still a huge win! They just committed to being interested in your help, and then to help you grow your business.

Win/Win.

After you complete your business, ask them who else do they know and love that can benefit from the services you have just provided for them. Zero downsides, all upside!

Win/Win.

Every so often, we suggest going back to the client to ask for more help to grow your business. Over time, they will have experienced how you operate, will recognize your integrity, and appreciate your gratitude for their assistance. Don't forget you are helping them release those endorphins! It may seem like a strange concept that as you ask for help from others, you are also helping them. However, having looked at yourself through the lens of our methodology, you can now better understand the way these processes occur in the brain.

Only one person is standing between you and your success... you! As soon as you decide to get out of your own way and begin to apply our simple strategy, that is when the magic begins! Be a trapper, remember? Now, off we go to the next powerful tool, *The Three Agreements!*

Chapter Seven

The Three Agreements and Your Word

After we teach *The Three Agreements*, you would not believe how angry people become. Yes, they get mad! Their anger stems from the fact that no one had ever taught them about this practical and straightforward approach earlier in their careers. It's always surprising for us to hear this because we feel everyone should already know these basic principles. Boy, were we wrong! You can't imagine how many times we hear, *"You mean delivering 'The Three Agreements' is all I needed to do to generate perpetual referrals in my business? But surely it must be more complicated than that!"* The real wonder is how *"The Three Agreements"* have been kept a secret from an industry for many years.

So, we have decided to write this book and make this information and our methods available to you! Now it's time to introduce you to *The Three Agreements*.

The *Three Agreements*, in simple terms, is a **closing strategy – The Three Agreements Close**. It is the tool we use to ask for business from our clients. We guarantee you this approach is a radically different and easier way to ask for business than other tactics you may have used in the past. You don't need to take our word for this; you will soon see it with your own eyes.

By using *The Three Agreements*, you automatically lower the defenses of your clients. Not only will this approach give you a greater sense of confidence, but it will also help the client see that working with you will be beneficial to them. Win/win. Again, your specific industry does not matter as long as you are providing exceptional services, superior products, and helpful ideas to your clients. Later we will guide you to a powerful video sales training series, should you require additional help.

We strongly believe in a business model where you maintain a client base from which more revenue can always grow. While this is our business philosophy, it may not necessarily be yours. However, if you are genuinely interested in creating leverage and perpetual income from your business, repeat sales, cross-selling, and endless referrals, this is the easiest method to accomplish those goals.

The premise of *The Three Agreements* stems from our wholehearted belief in the good we do for others. We have the utmost confidence from our years of success as leaders in our industry, that we are doing right by our clients, and in turn, doing good for society as a whole. The power and impact of *The Three Agreements* are a testament to our commitment to altruism. Once you learn this method, you will see that this will become an invaluable tool to create growth, prosperity, and endless returns to your business and life. This might sound like big talk, but you will soon see for yourself why we believe so much in our system.

You may have noticed throughout this book that we often refer back to points made in previous chapters. We do this to reinforce certain core concepts that are essential to building your system. As we have said several times already: if you do not believe in what you do, no one else will either! *The Three Agreements* is the perfect way to establish confidence and trust between you and your client.

The great thing about *The Three Agreements* is that one can apply it to any industry; whether you are in financial services, direct-sales recruiting, banking, insurance, mortgages, medicine, or health - everyone can benefit from *The Three Agreements*. If your business involves an ongoing relationship with your clients, *The Three Agreements* is a perfect method for you.

We will assume for now that you are already proficient in basic sales skills. However, just in case you're not, here are a couple of key sales points to keep in mind to prepare your clients for *The Three Agreements Close*.

• You have built a good rapport with your clients without wasting time with too much small talk - especially about yourself.

• You have done a viable needs analysis/fact-finding assessment, and you now know precisely what your client's primary interests are, along with their dominant motivating factors.

• You presented solutions to address these primary interests and dominant motivating factors.

• You answered their questions and concerns to their satisfaction without overpromising.

• You are ready to get them to commit.

Enter *The Three Agreements Close*.

The following scenario shows *The Three Agreements Close* in the insurance and retirement planning industry. As you read the scenario below, try to imagine yourself as a bystander hearing how *The Three Agreements Close* sounds and works. If what you are about to read seems scary, harsh, or too over-the-top, you must understand where we are with the potential client at this point in the relationship and sale process. We are confident that our services are valuable to them and believe in what we are offering, as we have a proven track record of success. We are also aware of the fact that we will maintain long-term relationships with these people and present ourselves and our services accordingly. In many cases, we may be in the lives of our clients and vice-versa, for decades to come. Ask yourself if this is also true in your business, and if this is the way you approach your clients? If not, it should be.

Let's dive into the scenario.

In the following example, our agent is about to ask their client to "buy" our product. In this case, "buying" means signing an application for a retirement solution or life insurance product. Again, don't get caught up in the specifics of content in this example as it is tailored for our business.

Agent:

"That's how the program works, Mrs. Johnson. What other questions do you have?"

Mrs. Johnson:

"You've answered them all."

Agent:

"Ok, you just need to sign right here next to the 'x.'"

(Agent slides the agreement in front of Mrs. Johnson, and when Mrs. Johnson reaches for agreement, the agent pulls it back!)

Agent:

"Before you sign this, what is your understanding of the document you are signing?"

(Agent makes Mrs. Johnson repeat what she thinks she is agreeing to).

Let's pause for a moment and discuss what has happened up until this point. Unfortunately, people sign things every day without truly understanding what it is that they are signing. This is dangerous for a multitude of reasons, one of which is that they may not truly comprehend the commitments as stated in the agreement. Agreements to conduct business involve two parties, both of whom are required to keep commitments to one another and to themselves. Often when two parties sign an agreement, each party only thinks of what the other person is going to do for them, and less about what they must do to uphold the deal as well. To ensure this is not the case with our clients, it is imperative that they understand what they are agreeing to and what is expected from both parties before the agreement is signed.

Remember that our clients are the most important part of our referral system, so they must be clear and confident about the deal they are making and the services they are buying.

We also ask our clients to demonstrate that they understand what they are buying to protect the deal from the deceitful business practices of others. It is crucial that the client fully understand what they are buying because this knowledge is the best defense to protect them from competitors. Often, an unscrupulous salesperson would be glad to use confusion to undo your agreement with the client and misdirect them into a worse situation for monetary gain. If this is the case, a client who fully understands the deal they are making will be your best salesperson to deter any would-be detractors, and to keep their interests safe.

Lastly, it is essential that the client feels satisfied and comfortable with how we conducted ourselves throughout the signing process. If the client pressured because you tried to rush the signing process, it might create doubt and jeopardize the deal. Therefore, when closing the deal and signing an agreement with a client, transparency, clarity, and patience are your best tools to ensure positive and lasting results.

Now let's get back to Mrs. Johnson and our agent. You will notice that our agent takes a moment and intentionally withdraws the contract before Mrs. Johnson had a chance to sign it. Why would the agent risk interrupting the process when they had used their system successfully to generate the sale that they are about to close? The answer is simple. By giving the client some time to reflect before they sign, and asking them to verbally confirm their understanding of the commitments laid out in the agreement, you enable your credibility with the client to soar. They will feel that you are not just in it for a commission, or simply trying to sell something to them without regard for their well-being, but that you sincerely care about them - which is true!

By giving the client another opportunity to review the deal, we are providing them with a chance to ask questions they may not have earlier, maybe due to fear or embarrassment. This will help them save face and they will feel at ease because they are not being rushed. **REMEMBER: NO ONE likes a pushy salesperson. Pushy salespeople are LOUD and tend to repel clients.** You must also keep in mind that your job is not to make the sale and run out the door before the client has a chance to change their mind like a thief in the night. At this point in the sales process, you should be a calm, patient, and powerful professional, whose presence comforts the client.

Where we left off, our agent was closing the deal with Mrs. Johnson. What happens next is the real magic, so prepare to have your mind blown! Once the client has demonstrated their grasp of the agreement, our agent delivers *The Three Agreements Close*.

Let's return to see *the Three Agreements Close* in action:

Agent:

"Mrs. Johnson, before I will take you on as a client, you must agree to three things:

FIRST, *if a member of my team or I call you, please answer the phone or call us back as soon as possible. I promise we will not call to sell you anything. We would only be calling to inform you about potential changes, updates, or other relevant information regarding your account.*

SECOND, *you must agree to meet with my team or me at least once a year for a review of your plan. It is our responsibility to ensure the plan is still accomplishing all the goals you set out to achieve.*

THIRD, *you agree to introduce me to people you know and care about who may need the type of help you are receiving from me today. Do you accept these agreements?"*

Mrs. Johnson:

"Ok, sounds reasonable!"

Let's break down the rest of the scenario.

Don't you see the value of having these agreements in place before doing business?

Of course, you do.

You may have thought that your job was done once you got the client to say "yes" and follow through by closing a deal, making a sale, or getting a contract signed. However, regardless of the type of business you are in, the real work begins when they say "yes." Your job is not just to obtain the sale; it is fulfilling it. Your income does not stop once you receive the commission; the thing that guarantees your business continues is the referral. What better testimonial than a happy referring client?

You might have also wondered while reading the scenario above, *"Is it fair to ask your client to agree to these three things*?" The answer is that it is entirely fair if you deem yourself a true and worthy professional. If a client is not willing to agree to these three agreements, there is a higher chance you will have issues with them down the road. If they do not agree to these simple requests, it may be a sign that they are difficult to work with and do not see the value in keeping up their end of the bargain.

Let's address the third agreement first, introducing us to people they know and care about who may need the same type of help we are providing to the client.

Notice in the above example, we do not use the word "referrals." We use the phrase, "**introduce me to people they know and care about**" instead. Why does the third agreement exist other than to make you rich? Simple. Your job is to keep the promise to the person in front of you - your client. They are buying **your** commitment to deliver goods or services. Understand, your job is not necessarily to find new clients. Yes, it is a primary function of doing business, and unfortunately, what most people in business are relegated to spending too much of their time doing.

If the client asks you why they must agree to introduce you to their friends and family whom they think might benefit from your products, the answer is easy:

"My primary function, Mrs. Johnson, is to watch your back and keep the commitments outlined in the documents you have just signed. If I am forced to constantly look for new clients, kicking over rocks, that is time spent that I am not able to devote to you. You help me so that I can do better by you."

Who would argue with that?

First, making the client feel better about themselves by helping you, will, in turn, improve their health and well-being. It's the *Give Back Strategy* at work. Second, it's about the client and the benefits they receive from your services. This is another win/win situation for both you.

In our decades of using *The Three Agreements Close*, not one person has EVER said no. We also have never lost one deal because we asked someone to commit to them. Just like the blackjack game from chapter one, you cannot lose. *The Three Agreements Close* also tells your client that your time is as valuable, as theirs. It certainly is, and you must believe this! While there may be some people out there who disagree and reject *The Three*

Agreements or rescind a sale, so far, we have had a 100% success rate.

Remember that it took courage to step up to the table and take a seat in chapter one. The rules of the game seemed too good to be true. The same applies here to you. You must have courage to try *The Three Agreements*. After it works for you once, you will never struggle with it again!

Do we always get referrals? Yes, when we follow-up. On the other hand, if we do **not** follow-up, we do not get referrals! We do not require or push our clients to give us their list of people on the spot. The client should take the time to think about the people they want to put on their list. We know we will have more time with them when we deliver the product or service, or when we follow up to ensure they are pleased with the results of our business relationship. This is what they agreed to by accepting *The Three Agreements*.

At this point, you should have a better understanding of how allowing other people to help you is a real benefit to society, not just to your bank account. Keep in mind; you can design your own Three Agreements following the simple structure below.

The number one rule for *The Three Agreement Close* is: make sure you use the **THREE** agreements!

You may be asking yourself why three agreements and not ten or more? **The rule of "threes" is universal; so, don't work against it!** Two agreements are not enough, and four is too many. It's vital to make sure the "ask for help" part is the third agreement and is not given prior, because this order is key.

This is another example of allowing your client to give back. However, be careful, if you only put in the "ask for help" agreement, and you do not include the other two agreements, you risk the client perceiving you as a manipulator. This is the last thing you want your client to think. Your clients' trust and confidence are not only dependent on the quality of your products and services but also knowing the fact that you are a reliable and honest person. **The perception that your client has of you must be of the utmost importance.**

If you study *The Three Agreements* carefully, you will notice that the first two agreements are about actions we are taking **for the client**, not about actions we are asking the client to take for us. What you've done is create a 2:1 ratio, putting most of the onus to keep agreements on yourself. That is attractive to the client.

We need the client to keep the promises outlined in their agreement, and part of our responsibility is to assist them in doing so. As you know, a business agreement does not stay intact by merely waving a magic wand; there are continuing actions and obligations that must be executed by both parties. After all, it would be irresponsible of you to allow an agreement to falter because the client was lazy or unwilling to hold up their end of the deal. You must help keep the client on track and fulfill the agreement to its fruition. Like all other relationships you have in your life, your relationship with your clients must be nurtured.

Conversely, the third agreement is about allowing the client to help you. How exactly should one approach the creation and execution of the referral strategy? For our agents, the execution varies from agent to agent and team to team. Some agents have a leave-behind form with slots for relevant information such as name, contact information, and relationship to the client. Other agents will organically gather the information on their next visit with the client.

Although we have provided you with an example of how we deliver our Three Agreements, feel free to make it your own.

Regardless of your approach, it is imperative that you remind the client of their agreement to provide you with a list of their friends and family whom you may be able to help. We do this with a telephone call or an email reminding them of the next appointment.

A follow-up email to the client should look similar to this example:

Good morning Ms. Smith:

Just a quick reminder that we have an appointment to deliver your policy next Wednesday at 2:00 p.m. in your classroom. At that time, I will also collect the list of people to whom you think I could be of service.

Looking forward to our meeting!

-Don

Why make things more complicated by trying to build a face-to-face business through cold calling or spend a fortune on advertising and marketing schemes? You have the best source of new business sitting right in front of you - a new customer!

Having confidence and a deeply rooted belief in the good you do for others is the true secret to making *The Three Agreements Close* a success! Now is the time to learn the habits required to run and grow a thriving business!

You are about to meet your amazing business assistant, "BombShelly," a system to keep track of this massive growth! This fantastic tool will help your business to expand faster than you will be able to keep track of.

Chapter Eight

"BombShelly"

We are about to tell you another secret, and it is a big one!

We mentioned her name above; she is, "BombShelly."

Before we properly introduce you to her, let us dive into one of the primary reasons why four out of five businesses fail within the first five years of operation. While there may be several contributing factors that play a part in the failure of any given business, these factors can all be synthesized into one primary reason; it is peoples' failure to treat a business like a business!

Let us elaborate. You see, a business is nothing more than a system. Remember the meaning of **S.Y.S.T.E.M.?**

Saving You Stress, Time, Energy, and Money

Not only is it a system (all successful businesses follow a similar system), it is why they are successful.

We have identified two clear ideas to make your business successful, which are the following:

1) Activity

2) A system to turn an activity into money.

Repeat: Activity, and a system to turn an activity into money. (Note: You will see individual words in **bold** throughout this chapter. The words or terms in **bold** are the definitions as we use them in our system).

It is essential to have enough people to perpetually buy, agree, or partake in whatever it is that you are selling in your business;

this is what we call your **pipeline**. Your **pipeline** will create **activity**, and **activity** will supply the **raw materials** of your business. Let us draw an analogy to drive this point home. Say your business involves a factory. Like any productive factory, you built your business on a platform. The platform used in a factory is an assembly line. Let's start by looking at the reasoning for and the functionality of an assembly line. An assembly line forces movement; it has a beginning, middle, and an end.

In the previous paragraph, you will notice we used the words **raw material**. The **raw material** is unprocessed and unrefined matter. Raw materials enter at the beginning of an assembly line and are then moved along and processed with great intention and efficiency, until they reach the end of the assembly line as a finished product.

The finished product is what generates all the revenue in a business.

A smart business can recognize the right **raw materials** that will generate the best outcomes, which equals the most revenue. A successful factory also identifies the most efficient and fastest way to move the **raw material** to the end.

Each step in the assembly line is clear and purposeful. There is little wasted time and energy because, as they say, time is money.

Furthermore, every step in the process has a name and terminology that distinguishes and defines the exact purpose of any given step. Now, bring this analogy to your business.

The **raw material** in your business is what we refer to as a **contact**. A **contact** is the lifeblood of any successful business and must be clearly defined. A **contact**, as it relates to our business, is defined as follows:

Contact (n):

A person who helps us in our business.

We recognize that this is a broad definition, but this is intentional. A **contact** is not necessarily someone who we are trying to sell to turn into a **client**. We will provide a concrete definition for **client** shortly, but for now, let's stay focused on **contacts**. It is important to note that **contacts** are not always **clients**, but **clients** are always considered **contacts**. With that in mind, the primary function of any business that involves people buying from or joining your company is making new **contacts**.

Sounds reasonable, but there is more to it than that. Systems, remember?

You need to have a specific and measurable system to make and manage your contacts. The system built to make new contacts involves specific activities.

Activity is defined as:

Activity (n):

Specific, relative actions and movement, in a given timeframe, with the intent to make new contacts.

Activities happen outside the factory. That is where we mine our raw **materials; contacts**. The **contacts** we make outside the factory are then brought into the factory for processing. Repeat: A **contact** is a **raw material** that must enter our factory to be refined. **Contacts** are refined in our system into two products: **referral sources** and **leads**. A **contact** can be both but will always be one or the other. If a **contact** cannot be made into either, it should be removed from your factory.

Understand, we are not trying to be patronizing, we know you know the meaning of these words. We are merely bringing them to your attention to show you how they work and how we define and use them in the context of our system.

Below you will find the rest of our business definitions. Again, every part of your business system, your assembly line, needs a clear definition:

Referral Source (n:):

> A person who directs us to potential leads.

Lead (n):

> A person in your revenue pipeline.

A **Lead** is then refined or converted into a **client**.

Client (n):

> A person who buys from us.

A **client** is where your factory becomes monetized. Another important definition is **pipeline**.

Pipeline (n):

> The system of movement in business. It is to your business what a conveyor belt is to a factory. It creates a constant forward movement.

As people enter your business pipeline, they are converted into a **referral source, lead,** and/or **client**. It is critical to your business success, to implement an automated system that distinctly categorizes and tracks each person, step-by-step, through your factory. This is the only effective and profitable way to build and operate a successful business.

This all sounds rather obvious, right? Yet, we find most people who come to us for help don't have any systems in place at all. To create a smooth flow and rhythm, businesses must implement systems. This process must feel natural. If you are not experiencing a steady stream and rhythm in your business through the use of your system, you are doing something wrong! It is likely because your "factory" lacks the efficiencies necessary for success.

We can help you fix that, so stay with us.

Here is a diagram illustrating what an efficient business flow model looks like:

Sales Flow

Every part of your flow has a name and a specific purpose. Proper movement and flow are what make your factory successful by making it work for you. The factory we built for our team is the best we have seen in any industry.

BombShelly is the most exceptional financial and business technology system ever created! She is the factory used by our many companies, business owners, and thousands of sales professionals.

Imagine hiring the perfect executive assistant. She is not only fearless in her pursuit of success, but she also manages all the headaches of tracking your business flow all while being undaunted by any challenges that may arise along the way.

BombShelly is that perfect executive assistant! What is BombShelly, you may ask? She is our CRM, **CRM = Client Relationship Manager**. As you know, every business MUST have a **CRM**.

Let us explore the basic functions of a reliable and effective **CRM**. A good **CRM** must allow you to track and customize your sales flow. Your sales flow consists of **Milestones**. Historically, milestones were actual stones placed on a road or path, letting a traveler know how far they were from the next village. Each milestone was placed in order, meaning you obviously could not go from milestone four to milestone six. The same holds true today; you must also build **milestones** in your business and follow the system to achieve success on your journey. A **milestone** in the context of a business is a micro-system in your sales flow.

We mentioned before that for a system to work, it must be simple. BombShelly is simple and easy to use, which is why she works so well. She is also intuitive, and by this, we mean she can predict what our business leaders are thinking and anticipates their next moves. Beyond her simplicity, what makes BombShelly so unique is that she was built by sales professionals from the entrepreneurial, not the corporate world. When we built her, we were not concerned with trying to impress people who buy CRMs for a national "sales force," as she was not made for them. We built her to service and support an individual or small business who does not want to struggle with the daily operation and management of their business. That is what makes her truly special and stand out within the sphere of CRMs in the industry.

Though she was mainly built for sole proprietors, she has the capability to be scalable and grow with a business as it expands.

BombShelly is THE system. Without her, thousands of businesses we support would not only struggle to manage their business flow, in fact, they might not be able to stay in business at all. Thankfully for them, and for us, we have her by our side. We strongly encourage that you use BombShelly to support your business as well.

Let's take a closer look at the first step of operating your business; **activities**. The word **activity** is a noun. It will remain just a word and an abstract concept unless you put it into motion in your system. It is the first **milestone** to be set in one's business. Here is where we drop a big "bombshell" – one of the biggest secrets to our success is that we are not looking for clients!

Read that again.

Our **activities** are NOT designed to find **clients!**

Looking for **clients** is a noisy activity that turns so many people who would usually help us, against us. Trappers do not make noise, remember? If you review the diagram earlier in this chapter, you will see the flow of our system laid out for you. The system starts with **activities**. What is next? **Contacts!** Next comes, **contacts!**

Our teams are always looking for **contacts** because **contacts** are the lifeblood of our success! Again, by studying the workflow we have outlined, you will see that something happens to our **contacts** on the assembly line. They are converted into either a **referral source** or a **lead**. By strictly adhering to this process, we create a perpetual system of **contacts**, as opposed to the approach of the average, failed salesperson, who is constantly looking for or purchasing **leads**!

By using BombShelly to move **contacts** through the system, something more powerful happens for our agents because looking for **contacts** is a quiet way to hunt. It does not repel **contacts** and

clients; it attracts them. It makes no noise! Remember the trapper? The trapper uses a system, rather than waste time and energy on looking to eat the next thing that comes along.

Your **activities** find **contacts**, your **contacts**, through proper and efficient movement along your assembly line, may become **referral sources**.

Do you recall when we taught you *The Give Back Strategy?* This strategy should be applied to your **referral sources**. By not viewing or treating your **referral sources as leads**, the person's defenses remain down. **Referral Sources** are much more likely to open their warm network when they are not in your **lead** crosshairs. You understand the difference, right?

Do not forget, people are not stupid; they can smell and feel your intentions from a mile away. That is why it is essential not to see people as both a **referral source** and a **lead** at the same time! Keep your intentions and actions separate, and you will be more effective in the long run.

Notice, we said, "at the same time." It is important to make a clear distinction between the two definitions. When we are working with a person in our factory, it is clear where and who they are in our system at each point in the assembly line process.

We want to be explicit about this concept; a person we meet can be a **contact**, then a **lead**, then a **client**, and eventually a **referral source**, in that order. Our system allows for that movement, but we strongly advise you not to change the order of this flow.

A person can also be a **contact** and then just a **referral source**. We have a different way of managing that flow. In general, the crucial point is that we are efficient in how we handle the flow. Before we input people into our system, it must be clear the purpose and role each person plays. Assigning these functions at each step of the process is what makes the system efficient. When we have established and maintained this clarity, BombShelly can go to work, keeping people moving through the factory to generate massive revenue for your business.

We think of each person at each step of the metaphoric assembly line as serving a specific and particular function and role. If we were to overwhelm one person with three or four different classifications at once, we risk making them feel as though they are being taken advantage of or manipulated. As we have stated before, manipulated or taken advantage of is the very last thing we want someone we are working with to feel about us. The success of our system - our success, in general, is dependent on the trust of the people with whom we work. We achieve this by engaging in win/win relationships that are reciprocal, creating a healthy "Give Back" loop. Following this strategy ensures the best results for everyone. BombShelly is the perfect system to aid in managing the people you work with at every step as the relationships evolve and develop.

As you can see, we put great emphasis on the flow of our system. It does something most failed businesses do not do; it creates a perpetual warm market. When you build a referral-based business, by definition, you are creating a warm market strategy. There is nothing more powerful than being introduced into someone's life by their friends, relatives, or respected colleagues. This approach is a significant factor that contributed to our business's success.

We deal with businesses and salespeople daily who insist on doing things the hard way through cold market development.

Why?

Because these people have no problem being a so-called billboard for other peoples' businesses. They will spend a lot of time telling you about a movie they just saw and tell you that you must see it too. Then, they will go on and on about the new restaurant you need to try. These are the same people who insist on making their own businesses suffer by doing things the hard way via cold market development but have no problem at all generating revenue for strangers through their own warm market. And they do it for free!

You will no longer be one of these people. From now on, you are going to be a student of your business flow. You will invest significant time studying your **activities** and become a skillful, silent, and benevolent trapper. You will focus on pursuing the proper **activities** that will put you in front of the right **contacts**. You will always approach your contacts with specific intent, grooming them into **referral sources**.

Armed with *The Give Back Strategy*, many **referral sources** will want to know more for themselves, turning themselves into **leads**. This is gold! You will approach your referrals with a warm-market mentality; friend-to-friend and family-to-friend. Your firm belief will be that these referrals will soon become new **clients**, and effortlessly through a natural process, be converted into **referral sources**. Because of the mutually beneficial rewards of *The Give Back Strategy* loop you've initiated, you will have a friend for life! All of this is built on a platform of giving more than you get, to ensure the universe continually opens new doors for you.

Now, back to BombShelly. We have built the factory at our expense, so you don't have to. [10]

Chapter Nine

The Five Absolutes of Wealth

What's next?

Wherever you are on your journey to success, we want to share with you the five fundamental cornerstones of our business. Although these cornerstones may not be the same for your business, we highly recommend you build a framework and foundation to establish certain principles on how to conduct your business. These cornerstones keep our rudder pointed in the right direction, even during stormy weather. Conflict and setbacks happen to all of us. It is how we react and deal with the ups and downs, and how we conduct ourselves during these times, that matters. Strong character, ethical behavior, and honesty to yourself and your clients, even in times of hardship, are a must.

These foundational building blocks allow you to deal with any given issue calmly, find the right solutions, and will enable you to learn how to avoid these same pitfalls in the future. It may sound simple, but what often prevents most people from adequately dealing with adversity, is a lack of guidelines and principles to deal with problems. This is why we suggest you establish cornerstones for your business to guide you along the way.

Here are the five cornerstones of our plan for success:

Vision

It is always important to possess a clear vision of where you are going and what you want to accomplish. If we cannot see the vision and destination, then there is no way we can get there. With a clear vision of where we are going and what we want to achieve, we will always be able to see the big picture, even when times are rough.

Dream Big

We need to ensure that our dreams are large enough so that the dreams and ideas of our families, friends, partners, and teammates can fit inside, with unlimited room for everyone's dream to grow. Never put a limit on your dreams.

Many people have dreams so small that it's nearly impossible to enlist others to see their vision. Think of a fishbowl. If your dream is so small that it can "fit" inside a fishbowl, it cannot grow past a certain point outside of the glass. Your dream needs to exist in the ocean of potential and opportunity!

When we coach and consult people, we always ask how much money they want to make in the next twelve months. As you can imagine, most people answer with the proverbial $100,000 as their answer. Why do people consistently say this number? What does this number of $100,000 represent that makes people think or believe it is the ceiling to reach for? Why don't they aim higher?

One hundred thousand dollars is not a "big" dream. How do you expect to attract superstars to join your team and clients to buy your products when your dreams and goals are so low?

Now, we understand that $100,000 may be a lot more than you may have ever made prior to this point in your life, but one does not build a dream with finite and limited materials from the past. We build our dream with unlimited materials and possibilities from the future!

Ignore Naysayers

This cornerstone truly speaks for itself, and it is a room divider among family and friends. Buckle up; the ride is about to get bumpy. Although your family and friends love you and do not want to see you hurt or suffer; sadly, they often take this concern and apply it in the wrong way. Specifically, family and friends always seem to be there to "support" you in failure, but rarely are there to support you on your journey to success.

Read that again.

Like many people out there, your friends and family might not be risk-takers. But as we have mentioned in this book several times, calculated, well-thought-out, planned risk, with proper systems in place for success, will yield great rewards.

What you are doing might seem scary and painful to the people closest to you because they cannot imagine taking the same steps you are taking for themselves. You may have left what seemed to be a "secure," job to become an entrepreneur, who started their own business and became 100% reliant on yourself without the "safety net" the Naysayers need. Now, there is nothing wrong with needing a net; however, be careful because that net can become the impediment separating you from financial freedom. If there were no risk, everyone would try it. You must be strong and focused and keep your eye on the prize.

Build your own dreams instead of trading time for dollars building someone else's.

This concept of entrepreneurship may sound extraordinary to you, but to some of your friends and family, it may seem like a terrible idea. These emotions most likely come from a protective place and often are projections of their own hang-ups and limitations. They might be fearful of taking such a leap for themselves and feel their insecurities manifesting vicariously through you. If you were to hurry up and "fail," they might feel relieved, and you could quickly rejoin them in the comfort zone. We are not saying that they are bad people, as we know that most of these feelings come from the subconscious and therefore are not malicious.

You cannot allow their inability to separate your path from theirs to affect you. We believe that **they should support your journey to success and not your failure.** We see this daily in our business, where people are too afraid to even share their business concepts or ideas with their own family and friends. These people operate under a veil of shame, for fear of the Naysayers' opinions. We say this all must end today.

We are here to encourage you and tell you that you are going to do this for yourself. We firmly believe, as should you, that your friends and family are morally obligated to help in any way they possibly can to support you. You would do the same for them - if they were to ask you! Get off your behind and ask them for all the help and support you need! Don't be afraid!

That said, we will remind you once again, because we cannot emphasize this enough, to make sure you have systems for success in a place that you can articulate to them before you ask them for help. When we say dream, we are not using the term "pipe dream." In our case, our dreams are real, and we can clearly articulate them to anyone. They are tangible, big, and clear, not pie-in-the-sky or hypothetical. When imagining and realizing your dreams, they should be big and real, and you must take all the necessary steps to make them happen!

Our dreams are so well defined, thought out, and planned, that we can show them to any banker and get a loan, every time. They are specific, measurable, clear, and concrete dreams with systems in place to support them. Your dream needs to be the same. Let your people see your business plan, the metrics, the numbers, and show them your system for movement.

Remember not to be afraid to ask the opinion of those closest to you! If nothing else, this will allow these people to feel like they are part of the decision-making process and organically enrolls them into supporting your dreams. As we have stated before, there is no such thing as a self-made millionaire, regardless of any boasting you may hear to the contrary. It takes an army of supports to win the war on apathy and mediocrity. Enlist your army now!

Work Your A** Off!

It is time for you to stop relying on the cliché phrase, "Work smart, not hard." This is a cop-out. Yes, we encourage you always to work smart. This book is a manual for working smart. However, you must work hard too! Grind! Be that person who breathes rare air, who is **unwilling to fail**. You see, just "wanting" to be successful is not enough. Nearly anyone you might ask would say they "want" to be successful. Merely wanting something, even wanting it badly, is not sufficient motivation to drive behavioral change and motion towards real success.

Read this next part carefully: you can want something forever and never act on it. We are all guilty of doing this. You can want the steak, have the money to buy it, but decide on the chicken. The reasons "why "do not matter, the fact is, wants do not motivate action.

When you have a great NEED, that is when miracles can happen!

There have been times in all of our lives, when we needed the money, but didn't have it. Then something happened out of nowhere, and he money suddenly appeared. You might have called this a miracle, but in reality, it was the universe merely doing its job. It will always give you what you need, not just what you want.

Remember, success can be a need too! The problem is that most people view it as a want.

We can take hours explaining the "how's" and "why's" of this concept to you, but instead, we will put our money where our mouth is and show you.

We will now introduce you to the online sales training platform based on Don's best-selling book, "60 Seconds to Yes".

www.60SecondsToYes.com

On the "60 Seconds to Yes" website, you will find a detailed audio and video series that takes a deep dive into his methodology, which focuses on the psychology of sales. Before writing his book, Don invested months collaborating with many industry professionals, as well as psychologists and other experts, to study the human brain and find out how it works to develop the most effective and efficient sales techniques.

Below, we have provided you with a password for you to learn these invaluable techniques for yourself.

LOGIN:

af@60SecondstoYes.com

PASSWORD:

60Seconds

We are sure the first twelve videos will blow your mind. This series is a $1,000 value, and we are giving it to you for free! This is a good segue into our next concept.

Give Back

We are businesspeople who are successful, logical, and straightforward. That said, we have referenced the power of the universal law of giving several times in this book.

We want to make clear to you that we are not your typical "woo-woo" type of people, peddling some hippie-dippy, new-age bs. We do not like trust falls, nor do we consult the stars to determine what actions to take on any given day. However, we do believe wholeheartedly in personal growth. We know first-hand the power of giving. There is constant movement in the universe, both expanding and contracting motion based on what we are asking for and how much we give in return.

At different moments in our lives, we have fallen into the "scarcity mentality" trap. However, one cannot live in scarcity and abundance at the same time; we must choose one or the other. We say choose abundance every time!

Another reason for choosing to give is simple; the single quality that is the most transparent to others is generosity - when you give from the heart. A genuine desire to help and give to others will grow your success quicker than anything else. Remember to work with integrity and honesty. This will get you much further in life and business than being the slick, in-it-for-themselves, snake-oil-salesperson that repels everyone he comes in contact with. Attract your clients with kindness, and you will be rewarded generously in your business.

Terry stresses the importance of giving first to the people he trains and works with, urging them to start giving before they achieve wealth and success. Of course, it's easy to give when you have a lot, but giving when you have very modest means creates the space needed for massive returns. The giver's heart shares time, experience, money, resources, love, and companionship, with zero expectation in return.

Many people give, but they make sure there is a camera rolling to capture the "giving" for the world to see. Usually, this type of "giving" is meant only to satisfy this person's ego on social media. It often has very little to do with the act of giving or the benefit to the receiver and more to do with the giver trying to get attention for themselves. We do not want to diminish the good these people may be doing, but it is difficult to separate the deed from the PR received.

To finish the discussion on giving, the universal law of giving is real. It is not only about what you ask from the universe, but it is also equally important how you ask for it.

Do good first, frequently, generously, without any expectation of a return, and watch the miracles fill your universe!

Chapter Ten

Final Thoughts

What you have just read is a result of many years of struggle that led to success, wrapped up neatly in a short book. The failures were the greatest lessons. We didn't mention many here because you materialize that on which you focus. Our intention is for you to focus on the key components for achieving your dreams.

The fact is: ours is a simple system. Always ask for referrals, always use the *Three Agreements Close*, and always use BombShelly to ensure your business is continually moving and growing beyond your expectations. Make these three components your primary focus, and you cannot fail. If it worked for us and so many of our associates, we know it will work for you too!

Stay relaxed, confident, and powerful, and always believe what you do is truly a great benefit to society. This is the perpetual formula for success!

We want to conclude this book with our definitions of what commitment is, for it is commitment that powers the forces of success.

- Commitment is what transforms a promise into reality.

- Commitment is the words you speak boldly of your intentions and your actions, which speak louder than your words.

- Commitment is the stuff that character is made of; it is the power to change the face of things.

- Commitment is coming through time after time, year, after year.

- Finally, commitment is the daily triumph of integrity over skepticism.

There is no shortage of people in the world who will tell you that whatever you want to achieve cannot be done. We are here to tell you the truth; not only can it be done, but you will be the one to do it!

Friends, we are here to help you in any way we can, without any expectation in return.

Reference

[1] Post, S., & Neimark, J. *(2007). Why Good Things Happen to Good People: How To Live A Longer, Healthier, Happier Life By The Simple Act of Giving.* New York. The Doubleday Broadway Publishing Group, a division of Random House, Inc.

[2] Hopper, E. *Spending Money on Others Can Lower Your Blood Pressure.* Greater Good Magazine. {Internet} (2016, May 12). Retrieved from https://greatergood.berkeley.edu/article/item/spending_money_on_others_can_lower_your_blood_pressure

[3] Renter, E. *What Generosity Does to Your Brain and Life Expectancy.* {Internet} (2015, May 1).
Retrieved from:
https://health.usnews.com.

[4] Fowler, J., H. & Christakis, N., A. *Cooperative behavior cascades in human social networks.* Proceedings of the National Academy of Sciences of the United States of America, {Internet} (2010) 107(12) 5334-5338.
Retrieved from:
https://www.pnas.org/content/107/12/5334

[5] Poulin, M. J., Brown, S. L., Dillard, A. J., & Smith, Dylan M. (2013). *Giving to Others and the Association Between Stress and Mortality.* American Journal of Public Health, {Internet} (2013) 103(9), 1649-1655.
Retrieved from:
https://www.ncbi.nlm.nih.gov/pmc/articles/PMC3780662/

[6] Oman, D., Thoresen, C. E., & McMahon, K. *Volunteerism and Mortality among the Community-dwelling Elderly.* Journal of Health Psychology, {Internet} (1999) 4(3), 301-316.
Retrieved from:
https://journals.sagepub.com/doi/pdf/10.1177/135910539900400301

[7] Dunn, E. W., Aknin, L., B., & Norton, M., I. *Spending Money on Others Promotes Happiness*. Science {Internet} (2008) 319(5870), 1687-1688.
Retrieved from:
https://science.sciencemag.org/content/319/5870/1687

[8] Moll, J., Krueger, F., Zahn, R., Pardini, M., de Oliveira-Souza, R., & Grafman, J. *Human fronto-mesolimbic networks guide decisions about charitable donation*. Proceedings of the National Academy of Sciences of the United States of America, {Internet} (2016) 103(42), 15623-15628.
Retrieved from:
https://www.ncbi.nlm.nih.gov/pmc/articles/PMC1622872/

[9] Contie, V. *Brain Imaging Reveals Joys of Giving*. National Institutes of Health. {Internet} (2007, June 22)
Retrieved from:
https://www.nih.gov/news-events/nih-research-matters/brain-imaging-reveals-joys-giving

[10] Check out the many companies that benefit from BombShelley under our Grow Capital Stock ticker: GRWC.